New York City Travel Guide 2025

Parks and Outdoor Spaces With Map & Images,,Famous Landmarks,Best restaurants & cafes,Museums and Galleries,Afro-Caribbean rhythms,Street Art of Brooklyn

By

Carole J. Harvey

Copyright © 2024 Carole J. Harvey. All rights reserved.

No part of this publication may be reproduced, distributed, or transmitted in any form or by any means, including photocopying, recording, or other electronic or mechanical methods, without the prior written permission of the publisher, except in the case of brief quotations embodied in critical reviews and certain other noncommercial uses permitted by copyright law.

Disclaimer
The information provided in this book is for general informational purposes only. While every effort has been made to ensure the accuracy and completeness of the information contained herein, the author and publisher assume no responsibility for any errors, omissions, or changes to travel details, prices, or locations. Readers are encouraged to verify any information with local authorities or service providers before making travel decisions. The author and publisher disclaim any liability for any personal, financial, or travel-related losses or damages incurred through the use of this guide.

Trademark
All product names, logos, and brands mentioned in this book are property of their respective trademark owners. Any use of trademarks or brand names is for descriptive purposes only and does not imply sponsorship, endorsement, or affiliation by or with the trademark holder.

Table Of Content

Chapter 1. Welcome to New York City! — 5
   Overview of NYC — 5
   Why Visit The Big Apple? — 6

Chapter 2: Planning Your Trip — 9
   The best time to visit — 9
   Packing Tips for NYC — 11

Chapter 3. Getting to New York City. — 14
   Getting to New York City via plane — 14
   Travelling to New York City via train — 16
   Getting to New York City by Bus — 19
   Getting to New York City by Ferry — 23
   Getting to New York City via helicopter. — 26
   Book Helicopter Rides to New York City. — 28

Chapter 4. Getting Around the City — 30
   Subway and Public Transport Tips — 30
   Taxis, Rideshares, and Walking — 32

Chapter 5. Top Attractions — 36
   Iconic Landmarks: Statue of Liberty, Times Square — 36
   Times Square: The Heartbeat of New York City — 40
   Museums and Galleries: The Met, MoMA — 44
   The Museum of Modern Art (MoMA) — 49
   Parks and Outdoor Spaces: Central Park, High Line — 52
   The High Line — 57

Chapter 6. Exploring NYC Neighborhoods — 61
   Manhattan: Uptown, Midtown, Downtown — 61
   Brooklyn: DUMBO, Williamsburg — 65
   Queens, Bronx, and Staten Island Highlights — 69

Chapter 7. Where to stay? — 73
   Luxury Hotels — 73
   Budget-Friendly Options — 74
   Unique Accommodations — 76

Chapter 8. Cooking and Dining Experiences — 78
   Bagels, pizza, and hot dogs are classic New York City cuisine. — 78
   Best restaurants and cafes. — 80
   Cafe — 81
   Food Trucks and Street Food — 83

Chapter 9: Shopping in the City — 86
   High-end boutiques — 86
   Local markets and thrift stores — 88

Chapter 10. Cultural and Historical Landmarks — 92
   Broadway & Performing Arts — 92

Chapter 11: Things to Do in NYC — 99

Seasonal Activities & Events ... 99
Nightlife & Entertainment ... 101

Chapter 12. Tips For A Memorable Trip ... **106**
Safety and Etiquette ... 106
Etiquette in New York City. ... 107
Budget-Friendly Travel Tips: ... 108
Stay at budget-friendly accommodations. ... 109

Chapter 13. Frequently Asked Questions ... **112**
Common Queries About NYC Travel ... 112

Chapter 14. Conclusion ... **115**
Final Tips for Exploring the City ... 116

Bonus ... **118**
Bonus: Expert Photography Tips ... 118
Useful website. ... 120
Dear Readers, ... 123

Chapter 1. Welcome to New York City!

Overview of NYC

Stepping into New York City for the first time is like going into a movie. The buzz of bustle meets you as soon as you arrive, with yellow taxis roaring their way through packed streets and the talk of residents and visitors mixing into an ever-present symphony. It's the kind of location that overwhelms you in the greatest manner possible—bright lights, towering buildings, and an energy that is almost difficult to explain but memorable to feel.

My first vacation to New York City began with an awe-inspiring encounter in Times Square. The massive digital billboards illuminated the night, and the sheer mix of people—from street performers and artists to families and professionals—gave the neighbourhood its personality. It seemed as if the whole globe had gathered in one location.

Beyond the famous landmarks, it's the tiny things about the city that capture your heart. Walking around Central Park on a bright fall morning, I felt the tranquillity that only nature can provide amid mayhem. Watching a local musician play the saxophone while golden leaves fell around me was an unforgettable experience.

Walking around New York City's neighbourhoods is like turning through a book of other realities. In Chinatown, the streets are busy with the smells of dumplings and roasted duck, and in SoHo, cobblestone alleyways lead to sophisticated stores and galleries. Each neighbourhood has its flavour, and they all contribute to the varied fabric that makes New York City so distinct.

However, it is the people of New York City that make it unique. New Yorkers are as varied as the city itself, with artists, dreamers, immigrants, and hustlers all marching to the same rhythm. I recall being on the tube one day, surrounded by strangers, each engrossed in their world: a mother soothing her child, a guy in a suit reading his presentation and a lady playing the guitar. It seemed to me at the time that New York City is a location where everyone comes to seek something, and the city somehow inspires you to dream big.

New York City is more than simply a destination; it is an experience. It's hectic and beautiful, tiring and thrilling. And once you've been there, it leaves an impression on you, much like the memory of a first love that you can never shake.

Why Visit The Big Apple?

New York City, sometimes known as the "Big Apple," is more than simply a destination; it's an experience that will remain with you long after you leave. Few destinations in the world provide such a diverse rich of culture, history, and adventure all in one city. Here's why NYC should be at the top of your vacation bucket list:

A Global Icon for Culture and Diversity

New York City is commonly referred to as the world's cultural capital, and with good cause. It's a melting pot of almost 8 million people from all walks of life, representing nearly every nation on the planet. This variety results in an unforgettable cultural experience, from the bustling neighbourhoods of Chinatown and Little Italy to the Afro-Caribbean rhythms of Harlem and the colourful street art of Brooklyn. Each part of the city tells its tale, transforming New York City into a celebration of mankind in all its manifestations.

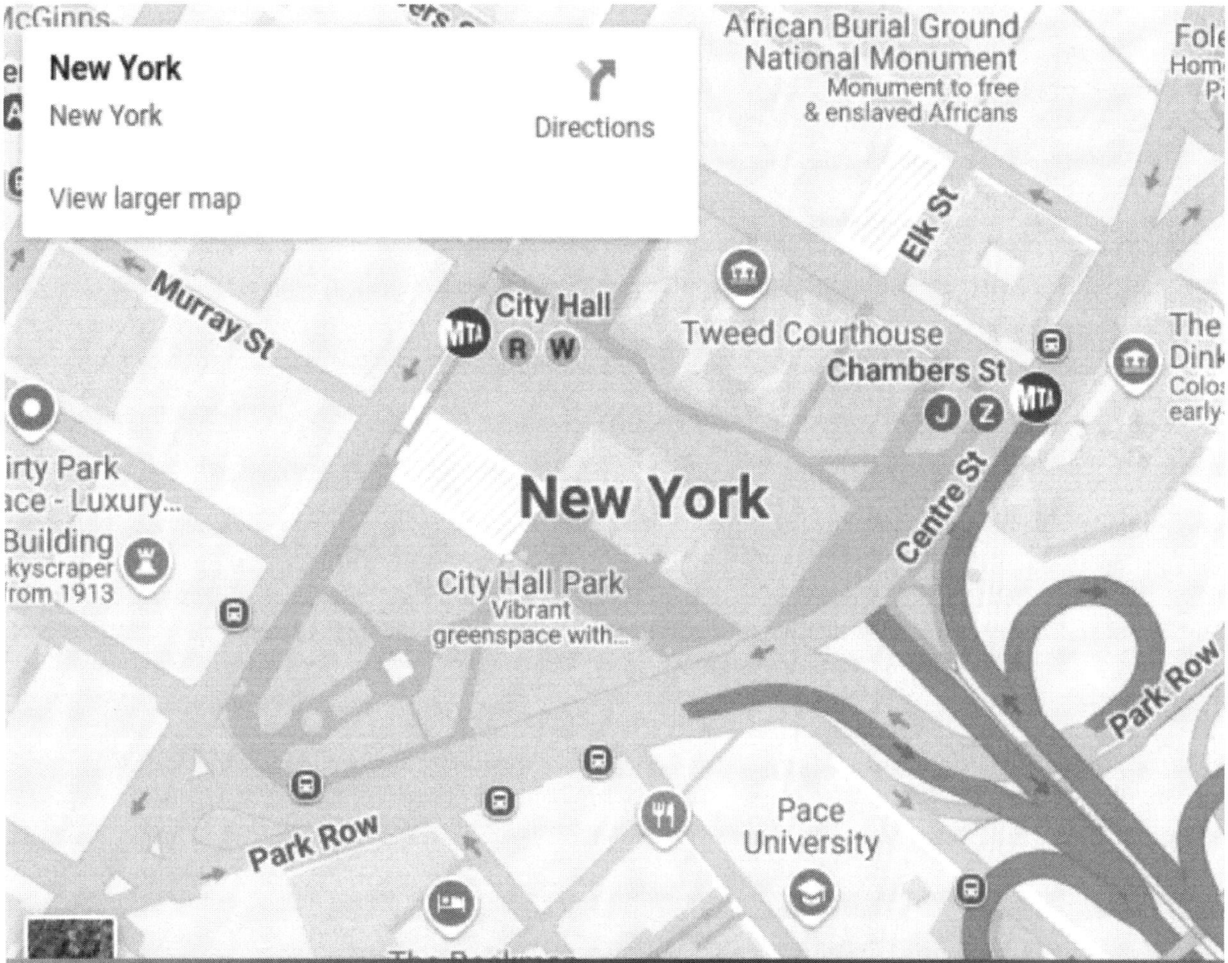

SCAN THE QR CODE

1. Open your device's camera app.
2. Align the QR code within the camera frame.
3. Wait for the code to be recognized.
4. Check the displayed notification or link.
5. Tap to access the linked content or information.

World Famous Landmarks

When you visit New York City, you enter a city that has influenced the world's imagination. Iconic structures such as the Statue of Liberty, the Empire State Building, and the Brooklyn Bridge are more than simply tourist attractions; they represent freedom, ambition, and architectural excellence. Whether it's admiring the sparkling lights of Times Square or taking a boat journey to Ellis Island, the Big Apple has several must-see attractions.

Unmatched Arts and Entertainment

NYC is a creative paradise, with world-class theatre shows on Broadway and underground music scenes in the East Village. Catch a Tony Award-winning production, immerse yourself in classics at the Met or MoMA, or discover a street performance in Washington Square Park. The city never stops innovating, and there is always something new to explore.

A foodie's paradise

If you enjoy cuisine, New York City will treat you with its gastronomic marvels. From Michelin-starred restaurants to hidden gems, the city offers flavours from all over the world. Consider New York-style pizza, freshly baked bagels with cream cheese, juicy halal cart chicken, and fashionable fusion cuisines. Each mouthful is a journey, and the diversity will make your taste senses appreciate you.

A city with endless possibilities

New York City is a city where anything seems conceivable. It's a city that encourages ambition, whether you're admiring Hudson Yards' creative architecture or strolling through Wall Street's venerable corridors. Every nook of the city exudes possibilities, making it a playground for both dreamers and doers.

A Walk Through History

History is alive in New York City. Visit the 9/11 Memorial to honour perseverance, wander through Greenwich Village's historic neighbourhoods, or learn about immigrant experiences at the Tenement Museum. Every step in New York City seems like you're travelling through history, with tales of struggle, victory, and reinvention around every corner.

Energy You Cannot Find Anywhere Else.

Perhaps the most compelling reason to visit New York City is the energy. The buzz of morning commuters, the light of the city at night, and the rhythm of its streets all seem to pulse with life. Something is thrilling about being in a city that never sleeps; it's an experience you can't have anyplace else.

Whether you want to see the lights on Broadway, relax in Central Park, or discover hidden jewels, New York City will inspire you. There's nothing quite like the Big Apple—once you've been there, you'll understand why it has such a particular place in people's hearts.

Chapter 2: Planning Your Trip

The best time to visit

New York City is a year-round destination, with each season providing a distinct atmosphere and set of activities. The optimal time to visit is determined by your preferred weather, crowd levels, and activities. Here's a rundown of NYC's seasons, with their advantages and cons:

Spring (March-May)

Pros:

• The city comes alive with flowering flowers, especially in Central Park and the Brooklyn Botanic Garden.

• Mild and pleasant temperatures range from 50°F (10°C) to 70°F (21°C).

• Lower crowds compared to summer, making it simpler to visit popular sights.

Spring activities, such as the Tribeca Film Festival and St. Patrick's Day Parade, provide cultural highlights.

Cons:

• Weather may be unpredictable, with some days being cold or wet.

• Hotel costs increase as the season advances.

Summer (June-August)

Pros:

• The long days and mild weather (75°F to 90°F, 24°C to 32°C) make it perfect for outdoor activities such as rooftop bars, open-air concerts, and walks.

• Free activities include Shakespeare in the Park, SummerStage concerts, and outdoor movie evenings.

• NYC beaches, like Coney Island and Rockaway Beach, provide a fast getaway from the metropolitan heat.

Cons:

• During peak tourist season, popular sites such as the Statue of Liberty and Times Square have massive crowds.

• Hot and humid weather may be unpleasant, particularly for people not used to metropolitan heat.

• Increased costs for flights and lodgings.

Fall (September through November)

Pros:

• The ideal weather, ranging from 50°F (10°C) to 75°F (24°C), makes touring the city a pleasure.

Central Park and other green spots are lovely with autumn foliage.

• Lower crowds than in summer, particularly in September and November.

• Seasonal events include the New York Film Festival, Macy's Thanksgiving Parade, and Halloween activities.

Cons:

• During October, hotel costs may increase due to high demand.

• Additional layers may be needed during cooler nights.

Winter (December - February).

Pros:

The holiday season turns New York City into a magnificent paradise, with festive lights, window displays, and historic events like the Rockefeller Centre Christmas Tree Lighting.

• Ice skating rinks in Bryant Park and Central Park provide a typical winter experience.

• The cheapest months for flights and accommodation are January and February.

Cons:

• Cold temperatures (25°F to 40°F, or -4°C to 4°C) may be extreme, particularly with windchill.

• Snow and ice weather may make walking and sightseeing less pleasant.

• Some attractions may have shortened hours during the off-season.

When should you go?

For Mild Weather and Outdoor Beauty: Spring and autumn are wonderful seasons for visiting NYC's parks and neighbourhoods.

• For a magical holiday experience, visit NYC in December.

• For budget travellers, January and February are the most affordable months, but be prepared for chilly weather.

• For Summer Fun: If you can tolerate the heat and congestion, summer is ideal for outdoor activities and city life.

No matter when you come, NYC guarantees memorable experiences; nevertheless, recognising the benefits and drawbacks of each season will help you make the most of your stay!

Packing Tips for NYC

Packing Tips for NYC

Packing for New York City may be difficult, particularly with its unpredictable weather, crowded streets, and different activities. Here are some practical recommendations to help you pack effectively, ensuring a pleasant and elegant trip:

Dress for the season.

Spring (March-May):

• Pack layers, including light sweaters, cardigans, and a medium-weight jacket.

• Wear comfortable walking shoes, such as sneakers or attractive flats.

• An umbrella or rain jacket for unexpected spring rains.

Summer (June-August):

• Wear lightweight, breathable apparel, such as t-shirts, shorts, and sundresses.

• Bring a hat, sunglasses, and sunscreen to avoid the heat.

• Walk in comfortable sandals or sneakers, avoiding heavier footwear during hot weather.

Fall (September–November):

Pack layers, such as a jacket or coat for chilly nights.

In late autumn, use scarves and thin gloves to stay warm.

• For crisp fall hikes, use boots or closed-toe shoes.

Winter (December-February):

• A warm and insulated clothing is needed.

• Add thermal layers, gloves, scarf, and beanie to remain warm.

• Waterproof boots for snowy or slushy streets.

Essentials for Exploring the City.

• Comfortable shoes:

Because New York City requires a lot of walking, prioritise comfortable and long-lasting shoes. Even fashionable trainers will blend nicely in.

• A sturdy daypack or tote bag.

Use it to carry basics such as water, food, a map, or a light jacket. Avoid bringing large luggage since subways and streets might become packed.

• Reusable water bottle.

Stay hydrated without continuously purchasing bottled water. Many parks and attractions provide replenishment stations.

• Portable charger:

Your phone will be your lifeline for navigation, images, and applications, so don't let it run out of battery.

Smart Packing for City Adventures

• Weather-appropriate outerwear:

The weather in New York City may change suddenly, so take a jacket or coat even in the warmer months, particularly for chilly nights.

• Mix & Match Clothing:

Neutral colours and adaptable items will conserve baggage room while allowing you to dress up or down as necessary.

• Evening outfit:

Bring one dressier outfit for evenings out on Broadway, rooftop bars, or fine dining.

• Compact umbrella:

Rain showers are frequent and unexpected, so include a lightweight, travel-friendly umbrella in your backpack.

Accessories that you must have

• City map or navigation app:

Download maps or navigation programs such as Google Maps or Citymapper to help you navigate your way around.

• MetroCard/Transit Pass:

Purchase one when you arrive, however carrying a tiny wallet or cardholder for quick access is useful.

• Sunglasses:

Even in the winter, the sun in New York City may be bright, so bring a decent pair of sunglasses.

Travel Documents and Extras

• Identification and Credit Cards:

Carry just the cards you need and leave the rest at home. Keep your ID handy for age-restricted activities.

• Ticketing and reservations:

Print or save digital versions of attraction tickets, theatre reservations, and event passes.

• Cash and coins:

While most shops take credit cards, little cash payments are useful for gratuities, street sellers, and tube trips.

Packing Tips for Safety

• Anti-theft bag:

Consider carrying a crossbody purse with strong zippers to keep valuables safe, particularly in busy settings.

• Minimal jewellery:

To avoid attracting unneeded attention, use understated accessories.

Optional yet useful items.

• Travel guidebook or notes.

Having a concise guide or list of scheduled tasks might save time.

• Earbuds or noise-cancelling headphones:

Ideal for tube rides or a quiet retreat from the city's hubbub.

By packing intelligently and putting comfort first, you'll be ready to experience all NYC has to offer, from its busy streets to its hidden jewels. Keep it simple, practical, and weather-appropriate, and you'll have a fantastic vacation!

Chapter 3. Getting to New York City.

Getting to New York City via plane

Flying to New York City is one of the quickest and most convenient methods to get there, particularly if you're coming from another state or an overseas location. NYC has three main airports that serve the metropolitan region, making it accessible from practically anywhere in the globe. Here's what you need to know about flying into the Big Apple:

Major Airports Serving New York City.

John F. Kennedy International Airport(JFK):

• Location: Queens, about 15 miles southeast of Manhattan.

• JFK is NYC's busiest airport, handling most foreign flights. It provides direct flights to and from places across the world.

• Transport to Manhattan:

The AirTrain JFK connects to the underground (E, J and Z lines) and Long Island Rail Road (LIRR) for convenient transfers.

• Taxis and rideshares: A taxi journey to Manhattan costs a fixed fee (plus tolls and gratuities).

• Shuttle Services: Shared vans provide door-to-door service.

La Guardia Airport (LGA):

• Location: Queens, about 8 miles northeast of Manhattan.

• LGA predominantly handles domestic flights with a small number of foreign flights. It is the nearest airport to Manhattan.

• Transport to Manhattan:

Local buses, such as the M60 SBS and Q70 SBS, link to subway stations.

• Convenient access to Manhattan via taxis and ridesharing services.

• Private car services provide for speedier and more pleasant travel.

Newark Liberty International Airport (EWR):

• Location: Newark, NJ, about 16 miles southwest of Manhattan.

• EWR serves both local and international flights and is a popular alternative to JFK.

• Transport to Manhattan:

• AirTrain Newark connects to NJ Transit trains, which carry you to Penn Station, Manhattan.

• Taxis and rideshares are widely accessible but may take longer owing to traffic.

• Express buses provide direct service to Manhattan's Port Authority Bus Terminal.

Airlines Serving New York City

• Domestic airlines include American Airlines, Delta, JetBlue, Southwest, United Airlines, and more.

• International airlines include British Airways, Emirates, Lufthansa, Air France, and Qatar Airways, among others.

New York City airports serve as hubs for major airlines, providing frequent flights and vast route networks to provide flexible travel alternatives.

Tips for Flying into New York City.

• Book early: Flights to NYC may be costly, particularly during high vacation seasons. Booking early might help you get better deals.

• Consider your arrival at the airport.

• JFK Airport is perfect for international flights and connections.

The LGA is ideal for brief domestic travels.

• EWR may be a preferable alternative for travellers from the western United States or certain overseas locations.

• Consider NYC traffic while planning your trip, particularly during peak hours.

Navigating Airports

• Allow additional time for security and navigation at major, crowded airports.

• Follow signs to baggage claim and transportation, or ask airport workers for help.

• Use airport applications to get flight status, terminal maps, and dining/shopping choices.

Pros and Cons of Flying to NYC:

Pros:

• Short travel time, particularly for international and cross-country travels.

• Direct flights from almost any place in the globe.

• Multiple airport choices provide flexibility depending on location and airline preferences.

Cons:

• Airports may be overcrowded, particularly during holidays and peak travel times.

• Getting from the airport to Manhattan may be time-consuming and expensive.

Flying into New York City is often the first step in an adventure. Whether you arrive at JFK, LGA, or EWR, a range of transportation choices will get you to your destination quickly. With enough organisation, the process may be streamlined, laying the groundwork for an unforgettable NYC trip.

Travelling to New York City via train

Travelling to New York City by train is a relaxing, picturesque, and stress-free alternative to flying or driving. With great rail service linking the city to other regions of the United States, the train offers a unique way to arrive while avoiding airport crowds and road congestion. Here's all you need to know about travelling to NYC via train:

Major Train Stations Serving NYC

Penn Station (NYC)

• Location: Midtown Manhattan, 34th Street and 7th Avenue.

• Penn Station is the main rail station in NYC, servicing Amtrak, LIRR, and NJ Transit. It is one of the busiest stations in the United States, with links to major cities along the East Coast and beyond.

• Services:

Amtrak provides long-distance and high-speed trains to and from major cities such as Boston, Washington D.C., Philadelphia, and Chicago.

The Long Island Rail Road (LIRR) connects Long Island to Manhattan.

The NJ Transit (NJT) connects New Jersey with Manhattan.

• Facilities include restaurants, shops, restrooms, baggage storage, and access to nearby metro lines.

Grand Central Terminal (New York City).

• Located at East 42nd Street and Park Avenue.

Grand Central is a historic landmark and transportation hub for the Metro-North Railroad, connecting NYC to sections of New York State and Connecticut. It does not service Amtrak.

• Services:

Metro-North Railroad provides commuter train service to locations including New Haven, Hartford, and Poughkeepsie.

Facilities include shopping, restaurants, historical exhibitions, and tube access.

Amtrak Service to New York City.

Amtrak is the primary intercity train supplier for New York City, operating a variety of services to and from the city. Whether you're travelling from local cities or across the nation, Amtrak offers a pleasant, dependable, and picturesque route to New York.

• Major routes to NYC:

• The Northeast Corridor (NEC) connects New York City to Boston, Philadelphia, and Washington D.C. by fast and frequent trains (Acela Express for business travellers).

The Cardinal provides service from Chicago to New York City over the picturesque Appalachian route.

The Lake Shore Limited connects Chicago to NYC via Albany and Buffalo.

The Crescent runs from New Orleans to New York City, passing via Atlanta, Birmingham, and other Southern cities.

The Silver Service (Silver Meteor & Silver Star) connects Florida to New York City, including an overnight option.

• Travel time:

• The travel time from Boston to NYC is 4.5 hours.

• Washington, D.C. to NYC: 3.5 hours.

• Travel time from Philadelphia to NYC: 1.5 hours.

• Travel time from Chicago to NYC ranges from 20 to 24 hours, depending on the route.

• Ticket options:

• Economy Class offers comfortable chairs and enough legroom.

• Business Class offers priority boarding, more room, and access to lounges.

• First Class offers enhanced comfort, private cabins, and premium facilities.

Advantages of Travelling to New York City By Train

• Trains like the Amtrak Northeast Corridor provide scenic vistas of the East Coast, including the Hudson River and rural New Jersey.

• Trains provide greater space than buses or aeroplanes, with comfortable seating, tables, power outlets, and Wi-Fi on many routes.

• Trains provide a more calm and stress-free travel experience than airports, with shorter security lines, fewer delays, and convenient access to food and beverages.

• City Centre Arrival: Train terminals, such as Penn Station and Grand Central, are conveniently placed in Manhattan, allowing you quick access to cabs, subways, and accommodations.

• Trains are an environmentally beneficial option for long-distance travel.

How to book a train ticket.

• Use Amtrak's website or mobile app to purchase tickets, see timetables, and get real-time information.

• Tickets are available for purchase at station ticket counters or self-service kiosks.

• Third-party travel agents and booking sites typically offer discounted train tickets.

• Book tickets ahead of time, particularly during peak seasons, to avoid fluctuating rates.

Transportation from the train station to your destination.

• From Penn Station (Amtrak):

• Direct access to numerous subway lines (1, 2, 3, A, C, E) for convenient city transit.

• Taxis and rideshares are available 24 hours a day, 7 days a week, with direct access to hotels and neighbourhoods.

• Walking: Nearby sites like Times Square, Herald Square, and Madison Square Garden may be reached on foot.

• From Grand Central (Metro-North):

Subway: Access to 4, 5, 6, 7, and S lines.

• Taxis and rideshares provide convenient direct access to your location.

• Walking: Nearby Midtown Manhattan attractions are easily accessible.

Advantages and disadvantages of taking the train to New York City.

Pros:

• Convenience: Arrive immediately in Manhattan (Penn Station or Grand Central).

• Comfortable seating and mobility while travelling.

• Enjoy scenic views over longer routes like the Crescent or Cardinal.

• Eliminate airport hassles, including lengthy security lines, waiting hours, and probable delays.

Cons:

• Travel Time: Although quicker than driving, rail travel may be longer than flying, particularly for cross-country routes.

- Limited Routes: Amtrak does not serve all locations, so if you are travelling from a city without direct train service to NYC, transfers may be needed.

- Train tickets may be costly, particularly when ordered last minute or for premium seats.

Tips for a Smooth Train Journey.

- For long-distance or crowded routes, arrive at least 30 minutes before departure.

- Pack light: Although train baggage restrictions are more liberal than airlines, it's still recommended to travel light for ease of mobility.

- Bring Snacks and Entertainment: Amtrak offers food and beverage choices, but taking snacks, books, or entertainment might enhance your travel experience.

- Check train timetables for real-time changes, since delays may occur.

Travelling to New York City by train is a pleasant and picturesque way to get to the centre of the city. Whether you're travelling from a neighbouring state or cross-country, the rail experience may add a unique aspect to your vacation, providing a more peaceful and pleasurable option to flying.

Getting to New York City by Bus

Travelling to New York City by bus is a cost-effective and handy choice, particularly for those coming from adjacent cities or areas. Numerous bus carriers run routes to New York City, offering affordable choices for lone travellers, families, and groups. Here's all you need to know about travelling to New York City by bus:

Major Bus Companies Serving New York City.

Several reliable bus companies provide services to New York City, with varying facilities and pricing ranges. Some of the most popular suppliers are:

a. Greyhound

- Greyhound is one of the major intercity bus companies in the U.S., with routes connecting places throughout New York City.

Greyhound's primary terminal is situated at Port Authority Bus Terminal (PABT) in Midtown Manhattan.

Greyhound offers a variety of seating choices, including economy and luxury. Their buses are equipped with Wi-Fi, power outlets, and bathrooms for your convenience.

- Greyhound routes from Boston, Washington D.C., and Philadelphia normally take 4–5 hours.

b. Megabus

- Megabus, known for its inexpensive pricing, provides services to NYC from several locations around the US.

Megabus serves from many sites in New York City, including Penn Station and The Port Authority Bus Terminal.

• Megabus offers free Wi-Fi, power outlets, and comfy seats. They are notable for their inexpensive prices, with tickets beginning at $1 on certain trips if booked in advance.

Megabus provides speedy connections from surrounding cities such as Boston, Philadelphia, and Washington D.C., requiring around 4-5 hours.

c. BoltBus

• BoltBus is a cost-effective solution that provides direct service to New York City from many East Coast locations.

• BoltBus' primary terminal in NYC is The Port Authority Bus Terminal.

• Services: BoltBus provides Wi-Fi, power outlets, and ample seats. They are well-known for their affordable rates and easy scheduling.

• Travel duration varies from 4-6 hours, including popular routes from Boston, Philadelphia, and Washington D.C.

d. Peter Pan Bus Lines

• Overview: Peter Pan provides services in cities around the Eastern United States, including NYC.

• Bus Terminals: Peter Pan buses usually arrive at the Port Authority Bus Terminal in Manhattan.

• Services: The firm offers basic bus facilities like Wi-Fi and power outlets, with inexpensive pricing.

• journey time: Similar to Greyhound, journey duration might vary from 4 to 6 hours based on departure city.

e. FlixBus

• Overview: FlixBus is an international bus business that provides services to NYC from destinations in the US and Europe.

FlixBus stations in New York City include the Port Authority Bus Terminal and other sites.

• FlixBus provides clean, contemporary buses with facilities like as Wi-Fi, power outlets, and bathrooms.

• Travel time from locations like Washington D.C., Boston, and Philadelphia is 4 to 5 hours.

Major bus terminals in New York City.

Several major bus terminals serve as the arrival and departure hubs for intercity buses travelling to and from New York City.

a. Port Authority Bus Terminal (PABT

• Location: Midtown Manhattan, 42nd Street and 8th Avenue.

• Overview: NYC's busiest terminal, servicing several firms such as Greyhound, Megabus, BoltBus, Peter Pan, and FlixBus.

• The terminal offers several food choices, shops, bathrooms, and waiting places. It is also well linked to the underground system (trains A, C, E, 1, 2, 3).

• Convenient access to Penn Station, Times Square, and other popular sights.

b. Penn Station

• Location: 34th Street and 7th Avenue in Manhattan.

• Penn Station serves not just Amtrak and Long Island Rail Road passengers, but also Megabus, BoltBus, and other bus services.

Penn Station has food outlets, retail stores and convenient tube connections (1, 2, 3, A, C, and E lines).

• Convenient access to Midtown Manhattan, offering shopping and eating opportunities.

c. Other Locations

• Some bus routes offer pickup/drop-off points near Madison Square Garden, which is close to Penn Station.

• Intercity buses from Chinese or East Coast lines often stop in Manhattan's Chinatown. This location is recognised for its affordable alternatives, albeit facilities may be limited.

Bus Routes to New York City

Bus travel to New York City is most prevalent from places on the East Coast, although there are routes to NYC from other regions of the country and beyond. Common routes include:

• Travel from Boston, MA takes around 4-5 hours.

• Travel time from Washington, DC: 4-5 hours.

• The travel time from Philadelphia, PA is around 1.5-2 hours.

• The travel time from Baltimore, MD is around 3-4 hours.

• Travel from Richmond, VA takes around 6-7 hours.

• Travel time from Providence, RI: Approximately 4 hours.

• Travel from Hartford, CT takes around 3 hours.

Buses departing from places beyond the East Coast may take longer, with journey durations varying from 8 to 24 hours depending on distance.

Advantages of Travelling to New York City by Bus

• Affordability: Bus travel to New York City is affordable, with rates beginning as little as $1 on services like Megabus and BoltBus when booked in advance.

• Convenience: Buses provide direct lines with fewer connections, making travel simpler than flying or driving.

• Comfort: Modern buses include Wi-Fi, power outlets, air conditioning, and toilets for a pleasant travel experience.

• Convenient Access to City Centres: Buses stop at major sites including Port Authority and Penn Station, providing quick access to cabs, subways, and accommodations.

Buses are a more environmentally friendly mode of transportation than automobiles or aeroplanes.

Drawbacks of Travelling to New York City By Bus

• Bus travel is slower than flying or riding the train, especially for lengthy distances.

• Traffic Delays: Buses may have delays due to road traffic, particularly during peak hours, leading to unpredictable journey times.

Comfort: Although buses are typically pleasant, lengthy travels from places beyond the East Coast may be exhausting compared to other types of transportation.

• restricted facilities: Bus companies may provide fewer facilities, such as restricted seats or outdated coaches.

Tips for a Smooth Bus Trip to NYC

To get the greatest pricing and availability, purchase your bus tickets early, particularly during peak travel times.

To ensure a smooth boarding and security process, arrive at bus terminals at least 30 minutes before departure.

• Pack food and entertainment for lengthy bus rides, even if Wi-Fi is available.

• Check for Delays: Get real-time information on bus arrival timings, particularly if travelling during peak hours or in bad weather.

Many travellers find that taking the bus to New York City is a cost-effective and convenient choice. Multiple bus companies provide direct connections to main Manhattan terminals, making it a convenient and cost-effective option to see the Big Apple. Whether you're coming from neighbouring places or farther away, bus travel offers a pleasant and picturesque journey into one of the world's most interesting cities.

Getting to New York City by Ferry

Taking a boat to New York City is a unique and picturesque way to see the city, with breathtaking views of renowned monuments such as the Statue of Liberty, Ellis Island, and the Manhattan skyline. While ferries are not as popular for long-distance travel as planes, trains, or buses, they do provide a good mode of transportation for guests coming from local regions or other sections of the New York metropolitan area. Here's a detailed guide on going to New York City via boat.

Major ferry routes to New York City.

Ferries to New York City often originate in surrounding territories such as New Jersey, Staten Island, and other portions of the New York metropolitan area. There are other ferry services connecting NYC to Long Island and sections of Connecticut. Some of the important ferry services are:

Staten Island Ferry

Overview: The Staten Island Ferry provides a free and picturesque journey between Manhattan and Staten Island, making it one of the city's most renowned ferry services.

• The ferry leaves from Whitehall Terminal in Lower Manhattan towards St. George Terminal on Staten Island.

• Travel time is around 25 minutes one way.

• The Staten Island Ferry operates every 30 minutes during peak hours and every hour off-peak. It is open 24 hours a day, seven days a week.

• Facilities: The boat offers comfortable seats, bathrooms, and refreshments. Passengers may also enjoy the open-air decks, which provide stunning views of the Statue of Liberty, Ellis Island, and the Lower Manhattan cityscape.

• The Staten Island Ferry is free of charge.

NY Waterway Ferry

• Overview: NY Waterway offers commuter ferries connecting Manhattan to New Jersey destinations such as Hoboken, Weehawken, and Jersey City.

• Ferries connect New Jersey ports (Hoboken, Weehawken) to Manhattan locations, including the Port Authority Bus Terminal, Brookfield Place, Pier 11/Wall Street, and West 39th Street.

• Travel time between New Jersey and Manhattan varies between 5 and 20 minutes, depending on the route and traffic conditions on the water.

• Frequency: NY Waterway ferries operate every 10 to 20 minutes during peak commute hours and less often during off-peak periods.

• Facilities: The ferries provide indoor and outdoor seats, Wi-Fi, and air conditioning. Some boats include snack bars with drinks and light foods.

• One-way tickets cost $9-12, with savings for round-trip and monthly passes.

The East River Ferry (NYC Ferry)

• The NYC Ferry service connects neighbourhoods in Brooklyn, Queens, and Manhattan by several routes along the East River. This boat service is popular with commuters and visitors alike.

• The NYC Ferry connects Manhattan, Brooklyn, Queens, and Governors Island, with stations at Wall Street/Pier 11, DUMBO, Brooklyn Bridge Park, and Astoria, Queens.

• Travel time between stations normally varies from 10-30 minutes.

• Frequency: NYC Ferries operate throughout the day, with more frequent departures during peak hours and restricted service during nights and weekends.

• Facilities: Ferries provide indoor seats, open-air decks, bathrooms, and onboard concessions for food and drinks.

The boat charges $4 for a single trip and provides reduced monthly and 10-ride packages.

Ferry to Governors' Island

• Governors Island, a famous tourist site, is accessible by boat from Manhattan and Brooklyn. The island has gardens, art pieces, and stunning views of the Statue of Liberty and the skyline.

Ferries depart from the Battery Maritime Building, Lower Manhattan, and Brooklyn Bridge Park.

The boat voyage takes around 7-10 minutes.

• Ferries run from May to October, with service every 15-20 minutes throughout the day.

• The ferry voyage to Governors Island is free during specific months (usually from May to September). However, special events or after-hours may incur a fee of $3-5 per passenger.

Benefits of Travelling to New York City by Ferry

• Taking a boat to NYC offers stunning views of the city's skyline, renowned monuments like the Statue of Liberty and Ellis Island, and the picturesque New York Harbour.

• Convenience: Ferries are an excellent alternative for travelling to New York City from neighbouring states such as New Jersey or Brooklyn. Many ferry services have stations near significant Manhattan sites, making it convenient to visit renowned sights.

Ferry ports provide a more relaxed environment than packed metro stations or bus terminals, making the voyage more enjoyable.

• NYC's ferry system connects many boroughs, making it a great alternative for sightseeing or commuting.

• Environmentally friendly: Ferries are a greener option than automobiles and buses, lowering the city's carbon impact.

The disadvantages of travelling to New York City by ferry

Limited routes: While ferry services are accessible to and from crucial destinations including Staten Island, New Jersey, and sections of Brooklyn, there are fewer routes than other types of transit like buses and subways. Long-distance ferry travel is less prevalent than rail or aeroplane travel.

Weather factors, such as strong waves, snow, and cold temperatures, may cause delays or cancellations for ferries.

• Peak travel periods may make some ferry routes, such as the Staten Island Ferry, congested and uncomfortable.

• Cost: Some boats, such as the Staten Island Ferry, are free, while others may collect tickets, which may be costly if used often during your vacation.

How To Book Ferry Tickets

• Most ferry operators provide online ticket booking via websites or mobile applications. Purchase tickets in advance for the NYC Ferry and NY Waterway to save time and ensure a seat.

• Most ferry routes provide onboard or terminal ticketing.

• Frequent ferry travellers may buy monthly or multi-ride tickets for cheaper fares. This is perfect for commuters and visitors who want to use the boat many times throughout their journey.

Tips for a Smooth Ferry Trip to NYC

• Arrive early: While ferry terminals are less congested than airports or bus terminals, it's still recommended to arrive 15-20 minutes before departure, particularly during peak hours.

To minimise surprises, check ferry timetables and real-time updates since delays might occur during busy hours or in bad weather.

Dress appropriately: Ferries may be cold on the water, particularly in the evening or during cooler months, so pack a jacket or jumper if you expect to be outside.

• Enjoy the Ride: Take advantage of the ferry's scenic vistas and capture photos along the way.

• Be prepared for crowds on some ferry routes, such as the Staten Island Ferry, during high tourist seasons. Prepare for more crowds and plan appropriately.

Pros and Cons of Taking the Ferry to New York City.

Pros:

• A scenic and unusual way to see New York City from the ocean.

Comfortable and less stressful than other modes of transportation, like as buses or vehicles.

• Excellent for touring, particularly near prominent NYC attractions such as the Statue of Liberty.

- Located near key terminals in Manhattan, Brooklyn, and New Jersey, providing easy access across the city.

Cons:

Limited service compared to other modes of transportation, particularly for people travelling from a distance.

- Weather may disrupt ferry timetables, resulting in delays or cancellations.

- Can be busy at peak travel hours.

- Ferries are not always a realistic choice for those coming from distant destinations to NYC.

Taking a ship to New York City is a pleasant and scenic way to begin your stay. Whether you're travelling from a local area or taking a beautiful journey across the harbour, ferries provide a unique experience that enables you to observe the city from the sea while enjoying the comfort and convenience of a well-managed service.

Getting to New York City via helicopter.

Travelling to New York City by helicopter is the most luxurious and exciting way to see the city. Whether you're visiting for a special event, a business meeting, or just want to indulge, a helicopter trip gives a once-in-a-lifetime experience that combines speed with unparalleled aerial views of the city's prominent monuments. This means of transportation is often employed by wealthy travellers, executives, and people looking for a speedy and picturesque journey into the city.

Helicopter service to New York City

There are various helicopter services available to travellers wishing to visit New York City. These services are usually operated from adjacent sites like New Jersey, Manhattan, and Long Island, with helicopters flying into New York City or the surrounding areas.

Helicopter Service from New Jersey

- Helicopter services from New Jersey normally fly from Teterboro Airport (TEB) or Newark Liberty International Airport (EWR) and land at Manhattan heliports (e.g. West 30th Street or Pier 6).

- Flight time between New Jersey and New York City is around 8-10 minutes, depending on takeoff and landing places.

Helicopter Service from Long Island

- Helicopters flying from Long Island's Republic Airport (FRG) or Farmingdale fly to Manhattan and land at heliports such as East 34th Street Heliport or West 30th Street Heliport.

- The trip from Long Island to Manhattan takes around 25-30 minutes.

Helicopter Service from Manhattan

• Helicopter services are available from various locations in Manhattan, including HeliNY (from the West Side Heliport, located at Pier 6 in Lower Manhattan) and Blade Helicopters, which offers flights to John F. Kennedy International Airport (JFK) and LaGuardia Airport (LGA).

• Flight Time: Flights from Manhattan to New York City airports take around 5-10 minutes.

Helicopter routes and scenic flights

While most helicopter services focus on transportation to and from the city's airports, several carriers also provide spectacular views of New York City from above. These aerial trips often have breathtaking vistas of:

• The Statue of Liberty.

Empire State Building.

• Central Park

• Times Square

• Brooklyn Bridge

• One World Trade Centre.

• The Hudson River.

For those wishing to add a particular touch to their vacation, certain helicopter services provide private trips above these locations, providing a unique viewpoint of the city's architecture and scenery.

Book Helicopter Rides to New York City.

Helicopter Transfers (Airport to Manhattan)

• Helicopter transfers to New York City are normally scheduled in advance with helicopter charter firms. Reputable providers, such as Blade or HeliNY, enable customers to book flights online or using a smartphone app. Helicopter services from airports (such as JFK or Teterboro) are offered to customers with international or local flights who choose to avoid regular ground transportation.

• Cost: Helicopter transfers range from $150 to $250 per person for one-way service, depending on the route and operator. Private flights may be more costly, with fees ranging from $1,500 to $3,000 for each trip.

Helicopter sightseeing tours

• Booking Process: HeliNY and Liberty Helicopters provide sightseeing trips departing from Manhattan's heliports. These may be booked via the company's websites or at the heliport (though prior booking is encouraged during peak periods).

• Scenic trips typically cost $150-300 per person, with durations ranging from 15 to 30 minutes. Private tours for parties or special events are offered at a premium.

Benefits of Travelling to New York by Helicopter

• Helicopter transfers are the fastest method to reach New York City from its airports. While the normal taxi or ride-sharing journey may take an hour or more, a helicopter may get you to Manhattan in less than 10 minutes, saving you important time, particularly for business travellers.

• Exclusive Experience: A helicopter trip provides a VIP experience, making you feel unique from beginning to end. It's an excellent choice for individuals commemorating a milestone or want to make a statement.

• The helicopter offers breathtaking panoramic views. You'll receive a bird's-eye perspective of iconic locations like the Statue of Liberty, Central Park, the Empire State Building, and the enormous city skyline, making for a one-of-a-kind sightseeing experience.

• Convenience: Helicopters provide rapid transport between New York airports and Manhattan. Avoiding traffic and the bother of lengthy airport security lines might help you travel more efficiently.

Drawbacks of Flying to New York by Helicopter

• Cost: Helicopter transfers may be more costly than other transportation choices. While handy, the cost is too high for many travellers, particularly for frequent usage.

• Helicopter rides are largely weather-dependent. Flights might be delayed or cancelled due to inclement weather such as heavy rain, fog, or strong winds. If the weather is unfavourable, you should have flexible arrangements or other transportation choices.

Limited availability: Although helicopter services are offered from particular areas, they are less common than other modes of transportation such as railroads or buses. You may need to book in advance, especially during peak travel seasons.

• Helicopter flights in and out of New York City are restricted by safety and air traffic laws, with just a few heliports open to the public. This may restrict travellers' freedom and alternatives.

Helicopter Safety and Comfort

• The Federal Aviation Administration (FAA) requires helicopter operators to follow strict safety standards. Passengers may anticipate well-maintained aircraft and skilled pilots qualified to manage a variety of situations.

• Helicopters provide pleasant seats but have limited capacity. Larger parties or families may find the cramped environment less pleasant than other modes of transportation. Furthermore, noise-cancelling headphones are usually given to assist block out engine noise and provide a pleasant trip.

Tips for Taking a Helicopter to NYC

• Book early: Helicopter services may be in great demand, particularly during tourist season or significant events in the city. Booking in advance is required to assure availability and the best pricing.

- Always check the weather prediction ahead of time. If the weather seems bad, it's best to postpone or prepare an alternate mode of transportation.

- If taking a helicopter transport from an airport to Manhattan, bring your identification or flight confirmation since heliport security might be identical to airport security.

- Allow time for security checks at the heliport before boarding, since these are similar to airport procedures.

- Dress comfortably since helicopter cabins are tiny. Avoid carrying bulky bags or backpacks that may not fit in storage compartments.

Taking a helicopter to New York City is an amazing travel experience that combines luxury, speed, and breathtaking views of one of the world's most recognisable cities. Whether you're here for business, pleasure, or tourism, a helicopter trip offers a unique view of the city and assures that you arrive in style. While the cost is exorbitant, the experience is unparalleled for anyone wishing to add some excitement to their trip to New York.

Chapter 4. Getting Around the City

Subway and Public Transport Tips

Subway and Public Transport Tips in New York City

New York City's subway system is one of the largest, busiest, and most iconic in the world, providing a fast and affordable way to navigate the city. With over 472 stations across four boroughs, the subway network serves millions of passengers daily, making it an essential part of daily life in NYC. In addition to the subway, New York's public transport system includes buses, the Staten Island Ferry, and other services that make it easy to get around the city. Whether you're a first-time visitor or a seasoned traveller, here's a comprehensive guide to using the subway and public transport in New York City, including essential tips to help you navigate the system like a local.

Navigating the Subway System

The subway is the backbone of New York City's public transport. It operates 24 hours a day, 7 days a week, and can take you to nearly every corner of the city.

Subway Map and Lines

The Subway Map: The subway network is made up of 27 lines, each marked by a letter or number, and color-coded for easy identification. The map can seem overwhelming at first, but it's relatively easy to use once you understand the basics.

Lines: There are several lines servicing Manhattan, Brooklyn, Queens, and the Bronx. Major lines to be familiar with include the 1, 2, 3 (red), A, C, E (blue), B, D, F, M (orange), and L (grey). The 7 line (purple) connects Queens to Manhattan.

Express vs. Local Trains: Some subway lines have express services, which skip certain stations, allowing for faster travel. Local trains stop at every station on their route. Be sure to check the signs on the platform to know if the train you are waiting for is express or local.

Understanding Subway Stops

Subway stations are typically found on street corners or in basements of buildings. Once you arrive at a station, pay attention to signs indicating the direction of trains and the specific trains serving that platform.

Uptown vs. Downtown: The direction you travel depends on whether you're going "uptown" (north) or "downtown" (south). Ensure you're on the correct platform and heading the right way.

Fare Payment

MetroCard: The primary way to pay for the subway is with a MetroCard, a rechargeable card that can be loaded with a set amount of money or an unlimited ride pass. MetroCards can be purchased at vending machines in subway stations.

OMNY: NYC is gradually rolling out a contactless payment system called OMNY. You can pay directly with your smartphone, smartwatches, or contactless bank cards at subway turnstiles.

Cost: A single subway ride costs $2.90. You can also purchase unlimited ride MetroCards for 7 days ($33) or 30 days ($127), which offer great value for tourists who plan to travel frequently on public transport.

Tips for Riding the Subway

Stay Aware of Your Surroundings: The subway can get crowded, especially during rush hours, so it's important to stay alert. Be aware of your belongings, as pickpocketing can occasionally happen, especially on crowded trains.

Know Your Stops: Before boarding, make sure you're clear on your destination and stops along the way. Use your phone's map or a paper subway map for reference. Many stations also have electronic boards showing train arrival times.

Avoid Rush Hours: The subway gets especially crowded during the morning rush hour (7:00 AM – 9:00 AM) and evening rush hour (5:00 PM – 7:00 PM). If you can, try to travel during off-peak hours when the trains are less packed.

Let Passengers Exit First: When the train arrives, let people exit before you board. This will make it easier to find a spot, especially during peak hours.

Keep the Right Etiquette: Stand on the right side of the escalator if you're not walking, and give priority to those walking faster. In trains, allow space for other passengers to get on or off.

Mind the Gaps: There is often a gap between the train and the platform, especially in older stations. Be careful when boarding and exiting to avoid tripping or getting stuck.

Seats: In the mornings and evenings, finding a seat can be difficult. If you're standing, hold onto the poles or bars for stability, and make sure you're not blocking the aisles.

Buses in New York City

In addition to the subway, buses are another vital part of New York's public transportation system. With over 5,000 buses running throughout the city, they are an easy way to travel short distances or to areas not serviced by the subway.

a. Bus Routes and Stops

New York City buses run on a network of routes that cover every borough, with routes numbered for easy identification. MTA buses serve Manhattan, Brooklyn, Queens, and the Bronx. Look for signs at the bus stop indicating the routes serving that location.

Bus Stops: Bus stops are located at intersections, and the buses usually stop to pick up and drop off passengers at designated areas. Signs will display the bus route number and destinations.

Bus Timetable: Some buses operate on specific schedules, while others run on demand. Real-time updates for bus arrivals are available through the MTA website and apps like Citymapper.

Fare Payment

MetroCard/OMNY: Like the subway, buses use MetroCards for payment. Simply swipe your card at the farebox near the driver, or use OMNY if you're paying with a contactless device.

Cost: Bus fares are the same as the subway at $2.90 per ride. You can use the same MetroCard for both subway and bus rides, making it easy to switch between the two.

Useful Public Transport Apps

MTA Subway Map App: This official app provides real-time schedules, subway maps, and service updates. It's an essential tool for navigating the subway efficiently.

Citymapper: A popular app for navigating New York's public transport system, Citymapper helps you plan your route, with details about subway, buses, walking, and even bike options.

Google Maps: Google Maps is another great resource for real-time directions and updates for navigating the subway, buses, or walking routes around the city.

Using the Staten Island Ferry

The Staten Island Ferry is a popular and free ferry ride that connects Manhattan to Staten Island, offering stunning views of the Statue of Liberty and the New York Harbor. It's a great way to experience New York City from the water without spending a dime. The ferry departs regularly from Whitehall Terminal in Lower Manhattan and takes about 25 minutes each way.

Taxi and Ride-Sharing Services

Though not part of the traditional public transport system, taxis and ride-sharing services like Uber and Lyft are widely available in New York City. They're a good option if you're travelling with luggage or to places not easily accessible by subway or bus. However, taxis and ride-sharing services are usually slower and more expensive, especially during rush hour.

Cycling and Walking

New York City is increasingly becoming more bike-friendly, with dedicated bike lanes and bike-sharing programs such as CitiBike. Walking is also an excellent way to explore the city, particularly neighbourhoods like Manhattan and Brooklyn.

Getting around New York City via subway and public transport is both efficient and affordable, with a little planning. While the system can seem intimidating at first, it quickly becomes second nature with a bit of practice. Armed with the right tips and tools, you can navigate the city like a local, whether you're hopping on a subway, taking a bus, or enjoying the scenic Staten Island Ferry. So, embrace the ride, and let New York's public transportation take you wherever you need to go!

Taxis, Rideshares, and Walking

Taxis, Rideshares, and Walking in New York City

New York City is known for its extensive and efficient public transportation system, but taxis, rideshares, and walking also play key roles in getting around the city. Whether you're looking for a quick ride to a destination, prefer the comfort of a private vehicle, or want to take in the city's vibrant streets on foot, these options provide great flexibility for exploring the Big Apple.

Taxis in New York City

New York City taxis are iconic, and catching one can be a convenient way to travel, especially if you're heading somewhere outside the subway system or when you want to avoid the hassle of navigating public transport.

Finding a Taxi

Hailing a Taxi: Taxis can be hailed on the street in Manhattan and many parts of the other boroughs. Look for taxis with "TAXI" signs lit up on the roof. If the light is on, the taxi is available. You can also find them at designated taxi stands, especially near busy areas like Times Square, Grand Central Station, and airport terminals.

Taxi Apps: You can also use apps like Curb or Uber to hail a yellow taxi, which can be convenient when you're in less busy parts of the city or want to avoid waiting on the street.

Taxi Fares

Starting Fare: The base fare for a taxi in New York City is around $2.50, with additional charges depending on the distance travelled and time spent in traffic.

Additional Charges: Expect additional surcharges such as a $0.50 fee for trips in Manhattan, as well as a $1 surcharge during peak hours or when travelling to or from airports.

Taxi Tips: It's customary to tip your taxi driver 10–20% of the total fare. If you're travelling during peak hours, heavy traffic, or extreme weather, the tip might be slightly higher.

Pros and Cons of Taxis

Pros: Convenient, private, can be hailed directly on the street, relatively fast in areas with less traffic.

Cons: Expensive, especially during rush hour, traffic can be unpredictable, and taxis may be hard to find in less busy neighbourhoods.

Rideshare Services (Uber, Lyft)

Rideshare services like Uber and Lyft are incredibly popular in New York City due to their ease of use, convenience, and ability to provide rides to more specific or remote locations not directly accessible by public transport.

How to Use Rideshare Apps

Uber & Lyft Apps: Download the app of your choice (Uber or Lyft) and create an account. Both apps work similarly: you enter your destination, select the type of ride you want (Standard, Premium, XL, etc.), and the app will match you with a nearby driver.

Pick-up Locations: The app provides a map with nearby pick-up points and estimated wait times. When you're ready, the app will notify you of the car's arrival and its location.

Payment: Payments are made directly through the app via credit or debit card, with tips optional (but generally expected). Most services offer an option to split the fare if you're sharing the ride with others.

Rideshare Fares

Surge Pricing: One key thing to be aware of is surge pricing, which occurs during busy times, such as rush hour, bad weather, or special events. This means fares can increase by a significant margin during these times.

Typical Fares: A typical ride in the city can range from $8 to $20 for short trips, but longer rides or trips to areas outside Manhattan (like Brooklyn or Queens) may cost more.

Pros and Cons of Rideshares

Pros: Convenient, door-to-door service, easier than hailing a taxi, price transparency in the app, various ride options (e.g., UberPool for shared rides or UberXL for larger groups).

Cons: Surge pricing, wait times can vary depending on location, and rides can be more expensive than public transport, especially during peak times.

Walking in New York City

New York is a pedestrian-friendly city, and one of the best ways to experience its vibrant neighbourhoods and iconic landmarks is by walking. Whether you're strolling through Central Park or exploring the unique districts of Brooklyn, walking gives you a front-row seat to the city's culture and energy.

Best Areas to Walk

Manhattan: Walking in Manhattan is highly recommended, especially in neighbourhoods like Times Square, SoHo, Greenwich Village, and Chinatown. You can easily walk between major attractions such as Central Park, The Empire State Building, Broadway, and The Metropolitan Museum of Art.

Brooklyn: The Brooklyn Bridge offers one of the best walking experiences, with a stunning view of the Manhattan skyline. Walking around DUMBO and Brooklyn Heights provides an intimate view of the Brooklyn waterfront and brownstone homes.

Uptown and The Bronx: If you're interested in seeing a more local side of the city, walking through Harlem or exploring the Bronx Zoo and Yankee Stadium offers a glimpse into the city's diverse neighbourhoods.

Walking Tips

Comfortable Shoes: Given the city's vastness, you'll likely end up walking a lot, so make sure to wear comfortable shoes.

Stay Alert: New York City streets can be busy and chaotic, especially at intersections and during rush hour. Always be mindful of cyclists, buses, and cars, and follow pedestrian signals.

Walking Routes: Use apps like Google Maps or Citymapper for walking directions and distances between destinations. New York is a grid system in Manhattan, making it easy to navigate.

Pros and Cons of Walking

Pros: Free, flexible, great for exploring, and allows you to see the city's neighbourhoods up close.

Cons: Can be tiring, especially in bad weather or if you're walking long distances, and may not always be practical for getting to distant destinations.

Combining Taxis, Rideshares, and Walking

Often, the best way to get around New York City is by combining taxis, rideshares, and walking. For example, you can take the subway to a specific neighbourhood and then use a taxi or rideshare to reach a more remote location. Alternatively, you might take a taxi or rideshare to your hotel and then explore the area on foot.

Taxis, rideshare services, and walking are all excellent alternatives to the subway and public transport when navigating New York City. Each mode of transport has its advantages and is suited to different situations, depending on your preferences, the time of day, and your destination. Whether you're hailing a yellow cab, jumping into an Uber, or simply exploring the city's vibrant streets on foot, New York offers countless ways to move through its diverse and exciting neighbourhoods.

Chapter 5. Top Attractions

Iconic Landmarks: Statue of Liberty, Times Square

The Statue of Liberty: A Symbol of Freedom and Hope

The Statue of Liberty, an iconic symbol of freedom, democracy, and hope, stands proudly at the entrance to New York Harbor. Gifted to the United States by France in 1886, this colossal statue has become one of the most recognized monuments in the world. A visit to Liberty Island is a must for anyone travelling to New York City, offering not only a chance to admire the statue up close but also to learn about the history, culture, and ideals it represents.

What to Explore at the Statue of Liberty

When visiting the Statue of Liberty, there's more to explore than just the statue itself. The entire experience is immersive, offering insights into American history and the enduring symbol of liberty.

The Statue Itself

Height and Design: Standing at 305 feet (93 meters) from the base to the tip of the torch, the Statue of Liberty is a massive monument. The statue represents Libertas, the Roman goddess of freedom, and is holding a torch in her right hand, while holding a tablet inscribed with the date July 4, 1776 (the day the Declaration of Independence was signed) in her left hand.

The View: The statue provides some of the most breathtaking views of New York Harbor, the Manhattan skyline, and the Brooklyn Bridge. Visitors can enjoy a panoramic view from the pedestal and the crown (with advanced reservations).

Liberty Island Museum

The Museum: The Statue of Liberty Museum, located on Liberty Island, offers a fascinating exhibition about the statue's history, construction, and significance. The museum showcases historical artefacts, models, and multimedia presentations that take visitors through the journey of the statue's creation and its role as a beacon of hope for immigrants arriving in the United States.

Exhibits: Notable exhibits include the original torch that was replaced in 1984 and the model that inspired the statue's design. Visitors can also learn about the importance of the statue to American immigrants, as it was often one of the first landmarks they saw when arriving in New York City.

Pedestal and Crown Access

Pedestal: For those interested in getting a closer look at the statue, you can visit the pedestal, which has an observation deck with incredible views of the surrounding area. The pedestal itself is built atop a fortress and was designed by architect Richard Morris Hunt.

Crown Access: The crown offers one of the most exclusive experiences at the statue. Visitors who secure tickets in advance can climb to the top of the statue's crown, which provides a stunning 360-degree view of New York Harbor, Manhattan, and New Jersey.

How to Get to the Statue of Liberty

Getting to the Statue of Liberty involves a ferry ride from Battery Park in Lower Manhattan. The ferry service is operated by Statue Cruises, the official concessionaire for visits to Liberty Island and Ellis Island.

Ferry Departures

Battery Park: The ferry to Liberty Island departs from Battery Park in Lower Manhattan. It's easily accessible by subway (take the 4/5 to Bowling Green, or the 1 train to South Ferry).

Duration of the Ferry Ride: The ferry ride from Battery Park to Liberty Island takes about 15–20 minutes one way.

Combined Tickets: Ferry tickets to Liberty Island can be combined with tickets to Ellis Island (home of the Ellis Island National Museum of Immigration), which is a short ride from Liberty Island. This combination allows you to explore both islands in one visit.

Boarding the Ferry

Security Screening: Before boarding the ferry, visitors must go through security screening similar to airport procedures. Expect to wait in line during busy times, especially during peak tourist seasons (spring and summer).

Ferry Times: Ferries run throughout the day, with departures every 20-30 minutes. It's recommended to purchase tickets in advance, especially during the high season, to avoid long lines and ensure a spot on the ferry.

Alternative Routes

Helicopter Tour: For a unique perspective of the Statue of Liberty, visitors can take a helicopter tour over the city, offering aerial views of the statue, Manhattan, and the harbour.

Private Boat Rentals: Another way to reach the statue is by booking a private boat rental or a sightseeing tour that includes the statue, though these are more expensive than the regular ferry service.

Cost of Visiting the Statue of Liberty

The cost of visiting the Statue of Liberty varies depending on the type of ticket you purchase, as well as additional experiences like a pedestal or crown access.

Ferry Tickets

Standard Ferry Ticket (Round-trip):

- Adults: $23.50
- Seniors (62+): $18.00
- Children (4-12 years old): $12.00
- Children under 4: Free

This includes round-trip ferry service to Liberty Island and Ellis Island.

Pedestal Access

Pedestal Tickets: If you'd like to visit the pedestal, you need to reserve a specific ticket in advance.

- Price: $23.50 for adults, the same as the standard ferry ticket, but requires booking in advance.

Crown Access

Crown Tickets: Access to the crown is limited and requires booking in advance (at least several weeks ahead due to high demand).

- Price: $23.50 for adults, the same as the ferry ticket, but crown tickets must be booked separately through Statue Cruises, and tickets to the crown often sell out well in advance.

Note: The climb to the crown involves walking up 354 steps, so it may not be suitable for everyone.

Additional Costs

Audio Tours and Guided Tours: Audio tours are included with your ferry ticket. However, if you prefer a guided tour, there are options available, often starting at $20-$25 per person.

Souvenirs: Souvenir shops on Liberty Island offer a wide range of Statue of Liberty-themed items, from T-shirts and mugs to replica models. Prices vary, with typical souvenirs costing anywhere from $5 to $30.

Best Time to Visit the Statue of Liberty

The Statue of Liberty can be visited year-round, but certain times of the year offer a better experience than others.

Spring and Fall (Best Time to Visit): The weather is typically pleasant, with fewer tourists than in the summer months. Expect cooler temperatures and less crowded ferries.

Summer (High Season): Summer is the peak tourist season, with long lines and large crowds. If you visit during this time, plan to arrive early in the day to avoid the busiest times.

Winter (Off-Season): While winter can be cold, the crowds are thinner, making for a more peaceful and quieter experience. Some services may have reduced hours during this time, so check the schedule before you go.

Tips for Visiting the Statue of Liberty

Book Tickets Early: Crown tickets, in particular, often sell out months in advance, so book your tickets as early as possible to ensure access.

Wear Comfortable Shoes: If you plan to climb to the pedestal or crown, comfortable shoes are a must. The climb can be strenuous, especially to the crown.

Bring Water and Snacks: There are cafes on Liberty Island, but it's always a good idea to bring a water bottle and snacks, especially if you plan to spend several hours on the island.

Weather: Be prepared for weather changes. The island is exposed, so it can be windy, especially on the ferry ride. Dress in layers and wear sunscreen.

A visit to the Statue of Liberty is one of the most memorable experiences in New York City. Whether you're marvelling at its grandeur, exploring Liberty Island's rich history, or soaking in the panoramic views of the harbour, the statue offers an enriching experience for visitors of all ages. By planning your trip carefully, you can make the most of this iconic American landmark, immersing yourself in its symbolism, beauty, and history.

Times Square: The Heartbeat of New York City

Times Square, often called "The Crossroads of the World," is one of New York City's most iconic and vibrant landmarks. Known for its dazzling lights, massive digital billboards, and bustling energy, Times Square is a must-see destination for any visitor to the city. Whether you're walking through its bustling streets, catching a Broadway show, or simply people-watching, Times Square offers an unforgettable New York experience.

What to Explore in Times Square

Times Square is filled with a variety of attractions, entertainment, shopping, and dining options. Here's a breakdown of what you can explore:

The Bright Lights of Times Square

The bright, neon lights and massive digital billboards that fill the area are a defining feature of Times Square. These flashing lights create a visual spectacle that's best experienced at night when the entire area comes to life. The famous "Naked Cowboy" performer can often be seen entertaining tourists, adding to the area's lively atmosphere.

Broadway Theater District

Broadway is located just off Times Square and is home to some of the best theatres in the world. If you're visiting New York, catching a Broadway show is a must. Shows like The Lion King, Hamilton, Wicked, and many more make Times Square the centre of the American theatre world. For discounted tickets, you can visit the TKTS booth in Times Square to purchase tickets for same-day performances.

Ticket Prices: Broadway tickets can range from $50 to over $200 for top-tier seats, depending on the show and seating section.

New Year's Eve Ball Drop

Times Square is world-renowned for its New Year's Eve Ball Drop. Each year, thousands of people gather in the square to watch the famous Waterford crystal ball descend from a 230-foot flagpole, marking the start of the New Year. The event is televised worldwide, drawing global attention to Times Square.

Madame Tussauds New York

If you're a fan of celebrities, the Madame Tussauds Wax Museum in Times Square is an exciting attraction. Featuring lifelike wax figures of famous stars, athletes, and historical figures, it's a fun stop for families and anyone interested in celebrity culture. The museum also has interactive exhibits where you can pose with the stars.

Ticket Price: Around $40 per adult for admission.

The Times Square Museum & Visitor Center

This small museum located in the heart of Times Square offers visitors a glimpse into the history of the area. Learn about the cultural significance of Times Square and its transformation from a theatre district to a global icon. The Visitor Center provides free information, maps, and guides about nearby attractions.

Admission: Free

Shopping and Dining

Times Square is home to a variety of flagship stores, including M&M's World, the Disney Store, and the Lego Store, where you can find unique New York City-themed souvenirs. If you're in the mood for shopping, stores like H&M and Uniqlo also offer trendy fashion.

For dining, Times Square offers a mix of international cuisine, quick bites, and upscale restaurants. Popular dining spots include Junior's Cheesecake, offering their famous New York-style cheesecake, and The Hard Rock Café, a tourist favourite for rock memorabilia and American fare.

Times Square Public Spaces

Times Square is not just about lights and entertainment. The area also boasts several pedestrian-friendly spaces. The Times Square Pedestrian Plaza opened in 2009, allows visitors to take a break, relax, and people-watch in the middle of all the action. You'll find red steps that offer a great place to sit, rest, and take photos.

How to Get to Times Square

Times Square is located in the heart of Midtown Manhattan, and it's easy to reach via several transportation options.

By Subway

Times Square is served by several subway lines. The 1, 2, 3, N, Q, R, W, A, C, and E lines all have stops at or near Times Square. The Times Square-42nd Street station is one of the busiest subway stations in the city and provides easy access to the square from multiple points in Manhattan and beyond.

Directions: If you're coming from Lower Manhattan, take the 1, 2, or 3 subway uptown. From Brooklyn, the N, Q, R, or W lines are a good option.

By Bus

Numerous buses pass through the Times Square area. The M42 and M104 buses are two of the most common routes passing through Times Square, providing convenient access from other parts of Manhattan.

By Taxi/Rideshare

Taxis and rideshare services (like Uber and Lyft) are another convenient way to get to Times Square. However, due to heavy traffic in the area, it's recommended to use these options during off-peak hours to avoid long delays.

By Foot

If you're already in Manhattan, Times Square is very walkable. It's a short walk from iconic landmarks such as Broadway, Central Park, and The Empire State Building. Times Square is also close to Penn Station, where many commuters arrive by train.

Cost of Visiting Times Square

Times Square is free to explore, but there are costs associated with certain activities and attractions.

General Exploration

Cost: Free. Exploring Times Square, taking photos, and walking around the pedestrian plaza is completely free.

Broadway Shows

Ticket Prices: Broadway tickets range from $50 to $200 or more depending on the show and seating options. For discounted same-day tickets, visit the TKTS Booth for up to 50% off ticket prices.

Madame Tussauds

Ticket Prices:

- Adults: $40
- Children (3-12 years): $35
- Under 3: Free

Shopping and Dining

Cost: Depends on your preferences. Souvenirs at stores like the M&M's World or Lego Store can cost anywhere from $5 to $50. Meals can range from a quick snack for $5 to a sit-down meal at a restaurant for $20–$50 per person.

New Year's Eve Ball Drop

Cost: Attending the New Year's Eve Ball Drop is free, but the crowds are massive. VIP tickets and special access to nearby hotels or restaurants can range from $500 to $3,000 or more for premium viewing areas.

Tips for Visiting Times Square

Expect Crowds: Times Square is one of the busiest places in the world, especially during holidays, weekends, and after-hours. Be prepared for crowds, long lines, and noise.

Wear Comfortable Shoes: If you plan on walking around, be sure to wear comfortable shoes, as you'll likely be doing a lot of walking.

Arrive Early for Broadway Shows: To get the best seats and avoid last-minute rushes, plan to arrive at least 30 minutes early for your Broadway performance.

Visit After Dark: The full spectacle of Times Square lights up after dark. If you're looking to see the area at its most vibrant, come at night.

Safety: Like any bustling area, keep an eye on your personal belongings. Times Square can get very crowded, and pickpockets may be in operation.

Times Square is one of the most thrilling and vibrant parts of New York City. With its dazzling lights, world-class entertainment, shopping, and dining, it's a place where energy and excitement converge. Whether you're catching a Broadway show, exploring the shops, or simply soaking in the atmosphere,

Times Square offers something for everyone. The best part is, that you can enjoy it for free—just walking around and taking in the sights and sounds of the world's most famous intersection.

Museums and Galleries: The Met, MoMA

The Metropolitan Museum of Art (The Met)

The Metropolitan Museum of Art, or The Met, is one of the most renowned and largest art museums in the world. Located on the eastern edge of Central Park, it stands as a cultural and artistic landmark in New York City. With over 2 million works of art spanning 5,000 years of human history, The Met provides an unparalleled opportunity to experience diverse cultures, art movements, and historical periods. From Ancient Egyptian artifacts to European masterpieces, and contemporary art, The Met is a treasure trove of human creativity and history.

Brief Overview of The Met

The Metropolitan Museum of Art was founded in 1870 with the mission of providing access to art and culture to the public. It consists of three main locations:

The Met Fifth Avenue: The museum's main building, located along Fifth Avenue, houses over 2 million works of art across 17 curatorial departments. This is the most famous and visited section of the Met.

The Met Cloisters: Situated in Fort Tryon Park in Upper Manhattan, this branch is dedicated to the art, architecture, and gardens of medieval Europe.

The Met Breuer: Although the Met Breuer closed in 2020, its legacy continues through exhibitions and programs that explore modern and contemporary art.

The Met has a world-class collection that includes iconic works by artists such as Rembrandt, Vermeer, Van Gogh, and Picasso, alongside masterpieces from ancient civilizations, Asian art, American art, African art, and more. The museum also hosts rotating exhibits, special events, and educational programs, making each visit unique.

What to Explore at The Met

The Met is divided into various departments, each showcasing art from different periods, cultures, and regions. Here are some highlights:

European Paintings

The Met boasts an extensive collection of European paintings, with works by masters such as Leonardo da Vinci, Rembrandt, Vermeer, Goya, and Monet. The museum's American Wing showcases a collection of American art, from the Colonial period to the early 20th century, including famous works by John Singer Sargent and Winslow Homer.

Ancient Egyptian Art

The Met's Egyptian Art collection is one of the largest and most comprehensive in the world. Explore mummies, sarcophagi, monumental statues of pharaohs, and artefacts from tombs, offering insights into the rituals and lives of ancient Egyptians.

Greek and Roman Art

Discover sculptures, vases, and artefacts from the Classical world. Iconic pieces like the Statue of Athena Parthenos and the Venus de Milo offer glimpses into the grandeur of ancient Greek and Roman civilizations.

Costume Institute

Known for its annual Met Gala, the Costume Institute showcases the history of fashion with exhibitions dedicated to the work of designers, fashion history, and the relationship between fashion and art. Past exhibits have focused on designers such as Alexander McQueen and Christian Dior.

Arms and Armor

The Arms and Armor collection contains suits of armour, swords, shields, and other weaponry from different cultures and historical periods. Notable pieces include armour worn by European knights and Japanese samurai.

American Art

The Met's American Art collection spans the history of the United States, from the early colonial period through the 20th century. Highlights include works by Edward Hopper, Georgia O'Keeffe, and John Singer Sargent.

Modern and Contemporary Art

The Modern and Contemporary Art section features works from the late 19th century onward, with pieces by famous artists such as Pablo Picasso, Jackson Pollock, and Andy Warhol. The Met's collection of American modernism is particularly notable.

Musical Instruments

The Met also houses an impressive collection of musical instruments from around the world, with everything from early pianos and string instruments to drums, horns, and rare ceremonial instruments.

The Met Cloisters

For visitors interested in medieval art and architecture, the Met Cloisters is a must-see. Set in a peaceful park in Upper Manhattan, it showcases the art, architecture, and gardens of medieval Europe, including tapestries, manuscripts, and early Christian art.

How to Get to The Met

By Subway

The Met Fifth Avenue is easily accessible via public transportation. The 6 subway line (Green Line) stops at Lexington Avenue/59th Street, which is a short walk to the museum.

You can also take the 1, 2, or 3 lines to the 72nd Street Station and walk to the museum from there.

By Bus

The M1, M2, M3, and M4 buses stop near The Met Fifth Avenue. The M5 bus also stops at the 81st Street entrance, which is convenient for the American Museum of Natural History if you're combining visits.

For the Met Cloisters, the M4 bus provides access from the city to Fort Tryon Park.

By Taxi/Rideshare

Taking a taxi or rideshare service like Uber or Lyft is an easy option, especially if you're travelling with a group or have limited time. The Met is located at 1000 Fifth Avenue, at 82nd Street.

By Foot

If you're staying nearby or visiting Central Park, The Met is within walking distance. The museum is located right next to the park at Fifth Avenue and 82nd Street.

Cost of Visiting The Met

The Met is known for its suggested admission policy, which means visitors are encouraged to pay what they can afford. However, there is a standard entry fee:

The Met Fifth Avenue

Adults: $30

Seniors (65 and over): $22

Students: $17

Members: Free

Children under 12: Free

The Met Cloisters

Adults: $25

Seniors (65 and over): $18

Students: $12

Children under 12: Free

Suggested Admission

While The Met recommends these prices, visitors can pay less or more based on their financial situation. The museum's suggested admission allows you to experience the museum for a price that fits your budget. This pricing structure applies to both The Met Fifth Avenue and The Met Cloisters.

Special Exhibitions

Some special exhibitions or events at The Met may require an additional fee, typically ranging from $10 to $25 per person, depending on the exhibit.

Met Membership

For frequent visitors, the museum offers membership options, which provide unlimited access, discounts at the museum store and café, and invitations to special events. Membership starts at around $85 per year.

Tips for Visiting The Met

Plan Ahead: Given the vast size of the museum, it's wise to plan your visit and focus on a few key areas that interest you most. You can download a map of the museum from their website or use the Met's mobile app for easy navigation.

Free Tours: The Met offers daily guided tours of the museum. Check the schedule when you arrive for a more in-depth experience of the exhibits.

Take Breaks: The Met can be overwhelming in terms of the number of exhibits and the sheer size of the museum. Make sure to take breaks, relax in one of the museum's courtyards, or grab a bite at one of the cafés.

Best Time to Visit: Try to visit during the weekdays or early mornings on weekends to avoid crowds. The museum is especially crowded during school vacation periods and major tourist seasons.

The Metropolitan Museum of Art is a cultural institution that offers visitors an unparalleled chance to explore the breadth of human history through art. Whether you're fascinated by Ancient Egyptian artefacts, captivated by European masterpieces, or inspired by modern art, The Met has something for everyone. With its diverse collections, world-class exhibitions, and stunning architecture, a visit to The Met is a must for anyone visiting New York City.

The Museum of Modern Art (MoMA)

The Museum of Modern Art (MoMA), located in Midtown Manhattan, is one of the world's most influential and renowned art museums. It is dedicated to showcasing and preserving modern and contemporary art across a wide range of disciplines, including painting, sculpture, design, photography, film, and digital media. Since its founding in 1929, MoMA has played a pivotal role in shaping the appreciation of modern art and remains a must-visit for art lovers and cultural enthusiasts.

Brief Overview of MoMA

MoMA was established with the goal of fostering understanding and appreciation of modern art. Over the years, it has become home to an extraordinary collection of works from some of the most significant artists of the 20th and 21st centuries. Its permanent collection includes over 200,000 works of art, with notable pieces by Vincent van Gogh, Pablo Picasso, Andy Warhol, Frida Kahlo, Jackson Pollock, and Salvador Dalí, among many others.

The museum has gone through several renovations and expansions, most notably a major redesign completed in 2019, which enhanced the visitor experience and created more space for exhibitions. In addition to its iconic collection, MoMA regularly hosts temporary exhibitions, film screenings, and educational programs, making it a dynamic destination for both new and returning visitors.

What to Explore at MoMA

MoMA's collection spans the history of modern art, with highlights that are world-famous and some that may be discoveries for many visitors. Here are some of the key areas to explore:

Famous Paintings and Sculptures

MoMA is home to some of the most iconic works of modern art, including Vincent van Gogh's "The Starry Night", Pablo Picasso's "Les Demoiselles d'Avignon", and Salvador Dalí's "The Persistence of Memory". The museum also has important works by Jackson Pollock, Mark Rothko, and Andy Warhol, including his famous Campbell's Soup Cans.

Contemporary Art

The museum's contemporary art collection is vast and includes works from both emerging and established artists. Highlights include Frida Kahlo's "Self-portrait with Cropped Hair" and Jeff Koons' "Rabbit". The collection features art from around the world, exploring themes of identity, culture, and technology.

Film and Media

MoMA is home to an extensive collection of films and media art, and it frequently hosts screenings of classic and contemporary films. The museum also focuses on the history of cinema with a particular interest in avant-garde and experimental works.

Photography

MoMA's photography collection includes over 25,000 photographs by legendary photographers such as Ansel Adams, Dorothea Lange, and Cindy Sherman. The museum's photography exhibitions provide a deep dive into the evolution of the medium, exploring both historical and contemporary perspectives.

Architecture and Design

MoMA has an impressive collection of architectural designs and industrial design objects. The museum's design collection includes everything from furniture and household objects to cutting-edge technological designs. Iconic pieces include Eero Saarinen's Tulip Chair and Charles and Ray Eames' Lounge Chair.

Special Exhibitions

MoMA hosts rotating special exhibitions that explore specific themes or focus on individual artists or movements. These exhibitions are often a major draw and offer fresh perspectives on contemporary and modern art trends.

The Sculpture Garden

MoMA's Sculpture Garden offers an outdoor space where visitors can enjoy works by some of the most important sculptors of the modern era, such as Henry Moore and Alexander Calder. The garden is a peaceful space for reflection and appreciating large-scale sculptures in an open-air setting.

How to Get to MoMA

By Subway

MoMA is located at 11 West 53rd Street between 5th and 6th Avenues. The closest subway stations are:

- E and M trains: Fifth Avenue/53rd Street Station (a short walk from MoMA)
- B, D, F, and M trains: 47th-50th Streets/Rockefeller Center Station (also a short walk to the museum)
- N, Q, R, and W trains: 57th Street Station (a few blocks away)

By Bus

MoMA is easily accessible by bus as well. Several bus routes stop near the museum:

- M1, M2, M3, and M4 buses run along Fifth Avenue and stop close to the museum.
- M50 bus also stops at the 53rd Street station.

By Taxi/Rideshare

Taxis and rideshare services like Uber and Lyft are widely available throughout Manhattan. Simply request a ride to 11 West 53rd Street, and the driver will take you to the museum.

By Foot

If you're staying nearby or in midtown Manhattan, MoMA is within walking distance of many popular attractions, including Rockefeller Center, Central Park, and Times Square.

Cost of Visiting MoMA

MoMA operates with a standard admission fee, though they offer different pricing structures depending on the type of visitor. The pricing is as follows:

General Admission

Adults: $25

Seniors (65 and over): $18

Students: $14

Children under 16: Free

MoMA Members

Members receive free admission to the museum, along with other perks such as discounts at the museum store and café, and access to exclusive events. Membership starts at $85 per year.

Free Admission

MoMA offers free admission on Fridays from 5:30 PM to 9:00 PM. This is a popular time to visit, so be prepared for larger crowds during this window.

Certain community groups and individuals with specific needs may also be eligible for free admission.

Special Exhibitions

Some temporary exhibitions at MoMA may require an additional ticket. These can range from $10 to $25 depending on the exhibition.

Family Admission

Families with children under 16 can visit for free. Additionally, MoMA offers various family-friendly programs and activities designed to engage younger audiences in the world of modern art.

Tips for Visiting MoMA

Plan Your Visit: MoMA's collection is extensive, so it's wise to plan your visit ahead of time. Focus on the galleries or artists that interest you most, and use the museum's website or app for exhibition schedules and gallery maps.

Special Events: MoMA often hosts special events, such as film screenings, talks, and interactive workshops. Check the museum's calendar in advance to see what's happening during your visit.

Guided Tours: MoMA offers both self-guided tours via their app and guided tours. If you're interested in a deeper understanding of the artwork, consider joining a guided tour, which often explores key works in the collection.

Avoid Crowds: MoMA can be quite busy, especially on weekends and during tourist-heavy seasons. Visiting early in the morning on weekdays is a great way to avoid crowds.

Take Breaks: With so much to see, it's easy to become overwhelmed. Take a break in one of MoMA's cafes or enjoy a moment of reflection in the museum's spacious galleries or the sculpture garden.

The Museum of Modern Art is a must-visit destination for anyone interested in modern and contemporary art. From van Gogh's swirling stars to Warhol's colourful soup cans, MoMA's collections offer a comprehensive view of the artistic movements that shaped the 20th and 21st centuries. Whether you're an art aficionado or a casual visitor, MoMA's exhibitions, films, and programs make it a dynamic and enriching experience in the heart of New York City.

Parks and Outdoor Spaces: Central Park, High Line

Central Park

Central Park is the heart and soul of New York City, a sprawling urban oasis that stretches over 843 acres in the middle of Manhattan. Opened in 1858, it is one of the most famous and beloved parks in the world. With its lush green landscapes, tranquil lakes, winding paths, and iconic landmarks, Central Park offers a respite from the city's hustle and bustle, providing visitors with a perfect mix of nature, art, and recreation.

Brief Overview of Central Park

Central Park was designed by landscape architects Frederick Law Olmsted and Calvert Vaux, who won a design competition to create a park that would serve as a public space for all New Yorkers. The park is not just a space for relaxation but also a cultural hub, with performances, exhibitions, and events happening year-round.

Spanning from 59th Street to 110th Street and between Fifth Avenue and Eighth Avenue, Central Park provides a variety of activities and sights, from tranquil spots for picnics to bustling recreational areas with sports facilities. It's also home to several landmarks, including historic bridges, statues, gardens, and theatres, making it a perfect blend of nature and history.

What to Explore at Central Park

There's no shortage of things to do and see in Central Park, with areas and attractions designed for visitors of all interests:

Bethesda Terrace and Fountain

One of the most iconic spots in Central Park, the Bethesda Terrace offers stunning views of Lake and is famous for its beautiful Fountain. The area is also a popular spot for photos and often features live musicians.

The Mall and Literary Walk

The Mall is a wide, tree-lined pathway that leads to Literary Walk, where you'll find statues of notable figures like Shakespeare and Robert Burns. It's a peaceful place to stroll and admire the park's grand architecture and old-growth trees.

Bow Bridge

The Bow Bridge is a stunning, wrought-iron bridge that arches over The Lake, offering scenic views and an ideal photo opportunity. It's one of the most photographed spots in Central Park.

Central Park Zoo

Located in the southeastern corner of the park, the Central Park Zoo houses a variety of animals, including penguins, sea lions, and snow leopards. It's an excellent spot for families and animal lovers.

Belvedere Castle

Offering panoramic views of the park, Belvedere Castle is a small castle perched atop a hill. The castle also houses a weather station and a visitor centre, providing fascinating exhibits about the park's natural history.

The Ramble

The Ramble is a 38-acre wooded area filled with winding trails, streams, and diverse wildlife. It's a favourite spot for birdwatching and offers a quiet, more natural environment for those seeking escape from the busy city.

The Great Lawn

The Great Lawn is a large open field where visitors gather for picnics, sports, sunbathing, and concerts. During the summer, it hosts various events, including performances by the New York Philharmonic.

Strawberry Fields

A peaceful memorial to John Lennon, who was tragically murdered near the park in 1980, Strawberry Fields features a mosaic with the word "Imagine," inspired by Lennon's famous song. It's a place for reflection and is often visited by fans of his music.

Sheep Meadow

Once home to a flock of sheep, Sheep Meadow is now a wide, open lawn where people relax, play sports or enjoy picnics. It's a beautiful spot for people-watching with a backdrop of Manhattan's skyline.

Ice Skating and Boating

Wollman Rink, located at the southern end of the park, offers ice skating in the winter months, while The Loeb Boathouse provides rowboat rentals for a peaceful experience on The Lake during the warmer months.

How to Get to Central Park

By Subway Central Park is easily accessible by subway, with several stations around its perimeter:

B, D, and E trains: Stop at 59th Street/Columbus Circle Station (southwest corner of the park).

A, C, B, and D trains: Stop at 59th Street/Columbus Circle or 72nd Street Station (west side of the park).

N, Q, R, and W trains: Stop at 57th Street/Seventh Avenue Station (southeast corner of the park).

1, 2, and 3 trains: Stop at 66th Street/Lincoln Center Station (west side of the park).

By Bus Several bus routes serve Central Park, and most buses run along Fifth Avenue, Madison Avenue, and Central Park West, all of which provide easy access to the park's various entrances. Some of the most common bus routes include:

M1, M2, M3, and M4: Running along Fifth Avenue and Madison Avenue, they stop near the park's southern end.

M7 and M10: These routes run along Central Park West and provide access to the park's western side.

Taxi/Rideshare Taxis and rideshare services like Uber and Lyft are readily available throughout Manhattan. Simply request a ride to Central Park, and the driver will drop you off at one of the entrances around the park.

By Foot, If you're staying near the park, Central Park is within walking distance of several popular destinations in Midtown Manhattan, Upper West Side, and Upper East Side. Walking to the park can be a pleasant experience, especially if you're heading to a specific landmark.

Cost of Visiting Central Park

Central Park is free to enter and explore. There is no admission fee to access the park or enjoy most of its attractions. However, certain activities and attractions within the park may have associated costs:

Central Park Zoo

Adults: $14

Seniors: **$12

Children (3-12): $9

Children under 3: Free

Boat Rentals at The Loeb Boathouse

Rowboat Rental: Around $20 per hour (plus a deposit).

Canoe Rental: Around $15 per hour (plus a deposit).

Ice Skating at Wollman Rink

Adults: Around $18–$25 (depending on the time of year).

Children (under 11): Around $8–$10.

Skate Rental: Around $10–$15.

Horse and Carriage Rides

Horse-drawn carriage rides around the park are available for approximately $50–$60 for a 20-minute ride.

Event Tickets

Central Park hosts various paid events throughout the year, such as Shakespeare in the Park, summer concerts, and festivals. Tickets for these events may range in price from free to $100, depending on the performance.

Tips for Visiting Central Park

Wear Comfortable Shoes: Central Park is vast, and exploring its many trails, paths, and landmarks can involve a lot of walking. Comfortable shoes are a must!

Bring Water and Snacks: While there are food vendors and cafes throughout the park, bringing your water and snacks is always a good idea.

Be Aware of the Weather: Central Park can be quite hot in the summer, so make sure to wear sunscreen, a hat, and light clothing. In winter, be prepared for cold temperatures, especially if you plan on ice skating.

Plan Your Visit According to the Season: Central Park offers unique experiences in each season – spring with cherry blossoms and lush greenery, summer with concerts and outdoor activities, fall with beautiful foliage, and winter with ice skating and snow-covered landscapes.

Whether you're looking for a peaceful retreat, an active adventure, or a cultural experience, Central Park has something to offer everyone. With its blend of natural beauty, historical landmarks, recreational spaces, and art installations, it provides the perfect opportunity to escape the fast pace of New York City while still being at its heart.

The High Line

The High Line is one of New York City's most unique and innovative green spaces. It's an elevated park built on a historic freight rail line that runs through Manhattan's West Side. Stretching from Gansevoort Street in the Meatpacking District to 34th Street, the High Line provides an immersive urban experience, offering lush gardens, art installations, stunning views of the city, and a space to relax and unwind.

Brief Overview of The High Line

Originally built in the 1930s as part of an elevated railway to transport goods through the industrial area of Manhattan's West Side, the High Line was left unused after the railroad's closure in the 1980s. It was transformed into a public park in 2009, thanks to the efforts of Friends of the High Line, a community organization that worked with designers James Corner Field Operations and Diller Scofidio + Renfro.

The park offers an elevated perspective of New York, with winding paths, wildflowers, urban art, and seating areas, making it a popular spot for locals and tourists alike. The High Line brings together nature, architecture, and community in a way that's unique to this part of the city.

What to Explore at The High Line

There's much to explore along the length of the High Line, each section offering something different:

The Gardens

The High Line features a beautiful combination of native plants and wildflowers, arranged to resemble the overgrown beauty of the original rail line. The gardens change seasonally, with lush greenery in the spring and summer, vibrant colours in the fall, and stark beauty in the winter.

Art Installations

The High Line is home to rotating art installations, both permanent and temporary. Some installations are interactive, while others provide thought-provoking commentary on urban life, history, or nature. Keep an eye out for sculptures, murals, and exhibits that are scattered along the route.

The Views

The High Line offers stunning views of the city's skyline, the Hudson River, and surrounding neighbourhoods. The park's elevated position makes it one of the best spots to photograph the skyline, especially around Chelsea and Hudson Yards. Don't miss the view from the 16th Street Viewing Platform, which offers a unique angle of the city's architecture.

The Amphitheater

Located at the 14th Street Passage, the amphitheatre is a popular space for performances, live music, and outdoor events. It's a great place to relax, sit on the built-in steps, and enjoy the art, and music, or just watch people pass by.

The 10th Avenue Spur

At the park's northern end, the 10th Avenue Spur is a section of the High Line that has been preserved with its industrial character intact. It offers visitors a glimpse of the past, as this section is not as heavily landscaped as the rest of the park.

The Glass Bridges

The glass bridges along the High Line provide transparent platforms that allow visitors to look down at the streets below, adding an exciting architectural element to the experience.

The Design Features

The High Line incorporates several design features that reflect the blend of nature and urban life, including reclaimed wood decking, steel railings, and sections where the track bed has been preserved. The park's design highlights the industrial heritage of the site, which is part of its charm.

How to Get to The High Line

By Subway The High Line is easily accessible via subway stations near its entrances. Some of the most common subway lines are:

A, C, E trains: Stop at 14th Street and 8th Avenue Station (near the southern entrance at Gansevoort Street).

L train: Stop at 14th Street/6th Avenue Station (a short walk to the High Line's entrance at 10th Avenue).

1, 2, 3 trains: Stop at 14th Street and 7th Avenue Station (near the southern entrance).

By Bus Several bus routes stop near the High Line, making it easy to access the park:

M11, M12, M14, M34A: These buses run along 10th Avenue, 14th Street, and nearby streets, providing access to different parts of the park.

Taxi/Rideshare Taxis and rideshare services like Uber and Lyft can drop you off at the High Line's entrances. Common drop-off spots include the Gansevoort Street entrance or 30th Street near the Hudson Yards area.

By Foot, If you are staying nearby, you can easily walk to the High Line from neighbourhoods like Chelsea, Greenwich Village, or Hudson Yards. The park is located within walking distance of Chelsea Market, the Whitney Museum, and Hudson Yards.

Cost of Visiting The High Line

Visiting the High Line is free of charge. It's a public park with no admission fee, making it a great place to explore without any cost. However, there are a few optional expenses to consider during your visit:

Special Events

Occasionally, the High Line hosts special events, such as outdoor concerts, art exhibits, or workshops. While most events are free, some may require advanced reservations or have a small ticket fee.

Food and Drink: There are several food vendors and kiosks along the High Line, particularly near the 14th Street Passage and Gansevoort Street entrance. Snacks, drinks, and light meals are available for purchase. Expect to pay around $5–$15 for food and beverages.

Shopping

The Chelsea Market, located near the southern entrance of the High Line, offers various shopping options, including gourmet food stores, boutique shops, and art galleries. Prices vary depending on the shop.

Tips for Visiting The High Line

Best Time to Visit: Early mornings or late afternoons are ideal to avoid crowds. Spring and summer are the most popular times to visit, but the park offers different experiences each season, with vibrant flowers in the spring, summer greenery, colourful fall foliage, and snowy landscapes in the winter.

Wear Comfortable Shoes: The High Line is 1.45 miles long, so be prepared to walk. Comfortable shoes are a must.

Bring a Camera: With its unique design and stunning views of the city, the High Line is a photographer's dream. Make sure to capture the iconic views and art installations along the way.

Plan Your Visit Around Events: If you're visiting for a specific event, check the High Line's official website or social media for any updates on performances, art exhibits, or public events.Stay Hydrated and Bring Snacks: While there are food vendors, it's a good idea to bring your water and snacks to stay refreshed while walking the park, especially during the hotter months.

The High Line is a testament to New York City's ability to repurpose old infrastructure in innovative ways. Whether you're looking to enjoy a peaceful walk, explore public art, or simply take in the stunning views of the city, the High Line provides a unique and unforgettable experience. It's a perfect example of how urban parks can blend nature, art, and history, making it a must-visit spot for anyone exploring New York City.

Chapter 6. Exploring NYC Neighborhoods

Manhattan: Uptown, Midtown, Downtown

Manhattan: Uptown, Midtown, Downtown

Manhattan is the beating heart of New York City, with each of its neighbourhoods offering a distinct vibe, culture, and experience. From the luxurious Upper East Side to the bustling streets of Midtown and the artistic vibe of Downtown, Manhattan provides visitors with a wide range of activities and sights to explore. Here's a breakdown of what you can expect from each area and how to get there.

Uptown Manhattan (Upper Manhattan)

What to Expect: Uptown Manhattan is home to some of the city's most iconic attractions, from sprawling parks to upscale neighbourhoods. It's quieter and less crowded than Midtown or Downtown, offering a more residential feel while still boasting plenty of cultural attractions.

Central Park: A must-see, it stretches over 840 acres and offers a variety of activities like biking, picnicking, or visiting attractions such as the Central Park Zoo.

Harlem: Famous for its African-American culture and music, particularly jazz, Harlem offers historic landmarks like the Apollo Theater and soul food eateries.

Museum Mile: Located along Fifth Avenue, this stretch is home to some of New York's most prestigious cultural institutions, such as the Metropolitan Museum of Art, the Guggenheim Museum, and the Jewish Museum.

Cathedral of St. John the Divine: One of the largest cathedrals in the world, it offers incredible architecture and peaceful gardens.

The Cloisters: A branch of the Met, this museum focuses on the art and architecture of medieval Europe and is located in Fort Tryon Park.

How to Get There:

By Subway: Uptown Manhattan is easily accessible by subway. Common lines are:

•   A, C, D, B, 1, 2, 3 trains: These lines run through various parts of Uptown, with stops in neighbourhoods like Harlem (125th Street), Columbia University (116th Street), and Central Park (59th Street-Columbus Circle).

By Bus: The M1, M2, M3, and M4 buses run uptown along major avenues, including Fifth Avenue and Broadway.

By Taxi/Rideshare: Taxis and rideshares are easily available, especially in Midtown or Downtown. Expect to pay around $15–$30 for a ride from Midtown to Uptown, depending on traffic.

Cost:

Central Park: Free (some attractions, like the Zoo, may have an entrance fee of $14.95–$19.95).

Museums: Many museums have an entrance fee (e.g., the Metropolitan Museum of Art has a suggested donation of $25).

Harlem: Walking around Harlem is free, but meals or performances may vary in cost.

Cultural Sites: Prices vary for specific sites and activities but typically range from free to $30.

Midtown Manhattan

What to Expect: Midtown Manhattan is the most iconic part of the city, known for its skyscrapers, vibrant energy, and attractions that attract millions of visitors each year. It's the commercial heart of New York and where you'll find some of the city's most famous landmarks.

Times Square: The pulsating heart of the city, known for its neon lights, Broadway theatres, and constant activity. It's a must-visit for first-timers.

Empire State Building: An iconic New York landmark, offering incredible views of the city from its observation decks on the 86th and 102nd floors.

Broadway: The world's most famous theatre district, home to a wide range of shows and musicals.

Rockefeller Center: Home to the Top of the Rock observation deck, the Radio City Music Hall, and the famous ice skating rink (seasonal).

Grand Central Terminal: An architectural gem with a stunning main concourse and a great place to start exploring Midtown.

How to Get There:

By Subway: Midtown is well-served by multiple subway lines:

- 1, 2, 3, A, C, E, N, Q, R, W, F, M, 7 trains all serve various parts of Midtown.

- Grand Central Station and Penn Station are major transit hubs, with many subway lines converging at these locations.

By Bus: Buses like the M5, M6, M7, M20, and M104 travel through Midtown along major streets like Broadway, Fifth Avenue, and Sixth Avenue.

By Taxi/Rideshare: Midtown is easily accessible by taxi or rideshare, but expect heavy traffic. Fares usually range from $10–$25 depending on traffic.

Cost:

Times Square: Free (shopping, dining, and attractions like the Broadway shows will have varying costs).

Empire State Building: Tickets range from $44–$77 for general admission to the observation deck.

Broadway Shows: Tickets range from $40–$200+, depending on the show.

Top of the Rock: Observation deck tickets cost around $38.

Grand Central Terminal: Free to visit, but shopping and dining options vary in price.

Downtown Manhattan

What to Expect: Downtown Manhattan offers a mix of history, financial power, and trendy neighbourhoods. It's where New York's story began, and it houses significant landmarks like the Statue of Liberty, Wall Street, and One World Trade Center.

Financial District: Visit Wall Street and the New York Stock Exchange or explore the historic Trinity Church.

One World Trade Center: The tallest building in the Western Hemisphere, with an observation deck offering breathtaking views of the city.

Statue of Liberty & Ellis Island: Take a ferry to visit these two historic islands, where you can explore the Statue of Liberty and learn about the history of immigration at Ellis Island.

Battery Park: A beautiful waterfront park that provides views of the Statue of Liberty and a great place to relax.

Chinatown & Little Italy: These culturally rich neighbourhoods are packed with delicious food, historical landmarks, and vibrant street life.

How to Get There:

By Subway: Downtown is easily accessible from Midtown and Uptown via several subway lines:

- 2, 4, 5, 1, A, C, J, and Z trains serve downtown neighborhoods.
- South Ferry (for the Statue of Liberty ferry) is accessible via the 1 train.

By Bus: Buses like the M5, M15, and M20 service downtown, with several routes passing through Chinatown and Wall Street.

By Taxi/Rideshare: Taxis and rideshare services are readily available, with prices ranging from $15–$30 from Midtown, depending on traffic.

Cost:

One World Observatory: Tickets range from $43 for general admission to the observatory.

Statue of Liberty & Ellis Island: Ferry tickets are typically $23.50 for adults, with additional costs for access to the pedestal or crown.

Wall Street: Free to explore, but attractions like the New York Stock Exchange and Trinity Church may have limited access.

Chinatown & Little Italy: Walking around is free; food and shopping costs vary.

Exploring Manhattan means immersing yourself in the energy and history of New York City. Whether you're visiting Uptown for cultural institutions and scenic parks, Midtown for iconic landmarks and shopping, or Downtown for historical sites and modern skyscrapers, there's something for everyone. Public transportation options make getting around easy and cost-effective, while taxis and rideshares offer a more comfortable but sometimes pricier alternative. Enjoy the diversity and excitement of Manhattan, and take the time to experience each neighborhood's unique charm.

SCAN THE QR CODE

1. Open your device's camera app.
2. Align the QR code within the camera frame.
3. Wait for the code to be recognized.
4. Check the displayed notification or link.
5. Tap to access the linked content or information.

Brooklyn: DUMBO, Williamsburg

Brooklyn: DUMBO, Williamsburg

Brooklyn, New York's most populous borough, offers a vibrant mix of culture, art, food, and history. Among its many neighbourhoods, DUMBO and Williamsburg stand out for their distinctive character and appeal. Whether you're strolling through cobblestone streets, taking in incredible views of Manhattan, or enjoying the creative atmosphere, Brooklyn has plenty to offer.

DUMBO (Down Under the Manhattan Bridge Overpass)

What to Expect: DUMBO is one of Brooklyn's most scenic and trendy neighbourhoods, nestled between the Brooklyn and Manhattan Bridges. Once an industrial area, it has transformed into a lively hub filled with art galleries, cafes, boutiques, and restaurants. It's particularly known for its picturesque views of the Manhattan skyline and Brooklyn Bridge.

Brooklyn Bridge Park: A sprawling park along the East River offering stunning views of Lower Manhattan, the Brooklyn Bridge, and the Statue of Liberty. It's a great spot for picnicking, walking, and outdoor activities.

Jane's Carousel: A beautifully restored 1920s carousel located in a glass pavilion along the waterfront. It's a great place for families or anyone who loves nostalgic charm.

St. Ann's Warehouse: A renowned performing arts venue that hosts everything from theatre productions to concerts and art exhibitions.

Pebble Beach: A small, rocky beach where you can relax and enjoy the views of the Manhattan skyline.

DUMBO's Cobblestone Streets: These streets, especially around Washington Street, are famous for their classic New York charm, framed by the towering arches of the Manhattan Bridge.

How to Get There:

By Subway: DUMBO is easily accessible by subway. Take the F train to York Street or the A/C trains to High Street-Brooklyn Bridge.

By Ferry: You can also take the East River Ferry to the DUMBO dock. This gives you a chance to see the city from the water and is a great alternative to the subway.

By Taxi/Rideshare: Taxis and rideshare services are available and relatively inexpensive. The fare from Midtown Manhattan to DUMBO is typically $20–$25.

By Walking: DUMBO is just across the Brooklyn Bridge from Manhattan. A leisurely walk across the bridge provides magnificent views of the city and a perfect introduction to the neighbourhood.

Cost:

Brooklyn Bridge Park: Free to explore.

Jane's Carousel: Tickets for the carousel are around $2 per ride.

St. Ann's Warehouse: Prices for performances vary, but tickets typically range from $20–$50.

Pebble Beach: Free to visit.

Dining & Shopping: Prices at local cafes, boutiques, and restaurants will vary, but expect to pay $10–$30 for a meal at an average restaurant.

SCAN THE QR CODE

1. Open your device's camera app.
2. Align the QR code within the camera frame.
3. Wait for the code to be recognized.
4. Check the displayed notification or link.
5. Tap to access the linked content or information.

Williamsburg

What to Expect: Williamsburg is a hip and trendy neighbourhood in northern Brooklyn, known for its arts scene, vibrant nightlife, and eclectic mix of restaurants and shops. It offers an edgy, youthful vibe that draws visitors from around the world. Williamsburg is also home to a strong LGBTQ+ community and a burgeoning craft brewery scene.

East River State Park: This park offers scenic views of the Manhattan skyline and the Williamsburg Bridge. It's a great place for a picnic or a leisurely walk along the water.

Smorgasburg: A weekend food market that brings together some of the best street food vendors in New York. It's a must-visit for foodies looking to sample a range of local and international cuisines.

Street Art & Murals: Williamsburg is known for its vibrant street art, with large murals covering many buildings in the neighbourhood. Walking around gives you the chance to see some amazing works of art.

Music & Nightlife: Williamsburg has a thriving live music scene, with venues like Music Hall of Williamsburg and Brooklyn Bowl offering concerts and events.

The Brooklyn Brewery: One of the area's most famous craft breweries, where you can sample a variety of beers brewed on-site.

How to Get There:

By Subway: The L train is the main subway line serving Williamsburg. Take it to Bedford Avenue, the neighbourhood's main street, for easy access to shops, restaurants, and attractions.

By Ferry: The East River Ferry stops at North Williamsburg, providing access to the waterfront and beautiful views of Manhattan.

By Taxi/Rideshare: Taxis and rideshares are available and typically cost around $20–$25 from Manhattan, depending on traffic.

By Bike/Walking: Williamsburg is bike-friendly and accessible by walking, especially from the Williamsburg Bridge if you're coming from Manhattan.

Cost:

East River State Park: Free to visit.

Smorgasburg: Admission is free, but food prices range from $5–$15 per dish.

Street Art: Free to explore.

Music Venues: Tickets for concerts typically range from $10–$30.

Brooklyn Brewery: Tours and tastings usually cost around $15–$20.

Dining: Williamsburg offers a variety of restaurants, ranging from budget-friendly to upscale, with meals costing around $15–$40.

Both DUMBO and Williamsburg in Brooklyn offer distinct and exciting experiences. DUMBO is perfect for those who want to enjoy stunning views, historical landmarks, and a mix of art and nature, while Williamsburg is a great choice for those seeking a trendy, artsy vibe, along with fantastic food, music, and nightlife. These neighbourhoods are easy to access from Manhattan by subway, ferry, or taxi and are ideal for a day or evening of exploration in Brooklyn. Whether you're strolling along the waterfront in DUMBO or indulging in street food in Williamsburg, you're sure to experience the unique energy of Brooklyn.

Queens, Bronx, and Staten Island Highlights

Queens, Bronx, and Staten Island Highlights

While Manhattan is often the first destination for visitors to New York City, the boroughs of Queens, Bronx, and Staten Island each have their unique offerings, rich culture, and attractions that are well worth exploring. From sporting events to cultural institutions, parks, and historical landmarks, each of these boroughs provides a distinct flavour of the city. Here's a guide to what you can explore in Queens, Bronx, and Staten Island, how to get there, and the associated costs.

Queens

What to Expect: Queens is a culturally diverse borough, known for its neighbourhoods that represent ethnic enclaves from all over the world. From the international food scene to the arts and sports, Queens has something for everyone.

Flushing Meadows-Corona Park: This park is home to the famous Unisphere and offers a range of activities. It's also the site of the Queens Museum and Citi Field, the home of the New York Mets.

Museum of the Moving Image: Located in Astoria, this museum is a must for film buffs. It offers exhibitions on the history of film, television, and digital media, along with screenings and events.

Astoria: Known for its Greek community, Astoria offers some of the best Mediterranean food in the city, along with a thriving art scene, including the Noguchi Museum and the Sculpture Centre.

Long Island City: A growing cultural district with impressive modern art venues such as MoMA PS1, as well as waterfront parks with fantastic views of the Manhattan skyline.

Rockaway Beach: For a relaxing escape from the city, head to this beach, one of New York's most popular spots for surfing, sunbathing, and beach activities.

How to Get There:

By Subway: Queens is accessible by many subway lines. Popular routes include the 7, N, Q, E, F, R, and M trains that serve neighbourhoods such as Flushing, Astoria, and Long Island City.

By Bus: The Q44, Q58, Q19, and Q60 buses run through Queens and are a good option for exploring various areas.

By Taxi/Rideshare: Taxis and rideshares are available, but can be more expensive compared to the subway, with fares ranging from $20–$40 depending on where you're coming from.

By Ferry: The East River Ferry connects Long Island City to Manhattan and offers beautiful views of the waterfront.

Cost:

Flushing Meadows-Corona Park: Free to visit.

Queens Museum: General admission is around $8.

Museum of the Moving Image: Admission costs approximately $15.

Astoria and Long Island City: Free to explore, but expect to pay for dining and shopping, with meals typically costing $10–$30.

Rockaway Beach: Free, though transportation costs for getting there via subway or bus will apply.

Bronx

What to Expect: The Bronx is known as the birthplace of hip-hop and is home to important cultural and historical sites, including its world-famous zoo, botanical gardens, and iconic sports venues.

Bronx Zoo: One of the largest zoos in the world, it offers an expansive variety of wildlife and immersive exhibits. It's a family favourite and has multiple themed attractions like the Congo Gorilla Forest and Tiger Mountain.

New York Botanical Garden: A stunning garden with year-round events, seasonal displays, and special exhibits. It's an oasis of natural beauty in the heart of the Bronx.

Yankee Stadium: The legendary home of the New York Yankees. Even if you're not a baseball fan, the stadium tour and surrounding area are great for exploring sports history.

Little Italy in the Bronx: A vibrant neighbourhood with fantastic Italian restaurants and markets. This area hosts the famous Feast of San Gennaro every year, which celebrates Italian-American culture.

Wave Hill: A public garden and cultural centre with breathtaking views of the Hudson River and the Palisades. It offers seasonal gardening workshops, cultural events, and outdoor art installations.

How to Get There:

By Subway: The 2, 4, 5, B and D trains serve the Bronx, making it easy to reach destinations like Yankee Stadium (via the 4 train to 161st Street), the Bronx Zoo, and the Botanical Garden.

By Bus: Buses like the Bx12, Bx1, and Bx19 serve various parts of the Bronx and are a convenient option to get around.

By Taxi/Rideshare: Expect fares to be around $20–$40 from Manhattan to the Bronx.

By Train: The Metro-North Railroad serves the Bronx, providing a convenient option for reaching destinations like Yankee Stadium and Wave Hill.

Cost:

Bronx Zoo: Admission starts at $19.95 for adults.

New York Botanical Garden: Tickets typically range from $15–$30 depending on the season and events.

Yankee Stadium: Stadium tours cost around $25 for adults.

Little Italy in the Bronx: Free to explore, but meals and souvenirs can vary, usually around $10–$25.

Wave Hill: Admission is typically $8 for adults.

Staten Island

What to Expect: Staten Island is often overlooked by tourists, but it offers a peaceful contrast to the hustle and bustle of Manhattan. Known for its parks, historic landmarks, and great views, Staten Island is perfect for those looking to explore a quieter part of New York City.

Staten Island Ferry: This free ferry ride offers stunning views of the Statue of Liberty, Ellis Island, and the Manhattan skyline. It's an iconic experience that's free.

Staten Island Greenbelt: This expansive park system offers hiking trails, wooded areas, and opportunities to experience nature within the city. Popular spots include the Clay Pit Ponds State Park Preserve and High Rock Park.

Richmond Town: A historic village that preserves Staten Island's early history, featuring well-preserved buildings from the 17th century and a living history museum.

The Staten Island Museum: This museum offers a diverse range of exhibits, including natural history, art, and local history.

National Lighthouse Museum: Located on the St. George waterfront, this museum celebrates the history of lighthouses and maritime navigation.

How to Get There:

By Ferry: The Staten Island Ferry is the best way to get to Staten Island from Manhattan. It departs from Whitehall Street in Lower Manhattan and is free.

By Subway: The 1 train runs to South Ferry in Manhattan, where you can take the Staten Island Ferry.

By Bus: The S40, S46, and S51 buses connect Staten Island to other boroughs and its neighbourhoods.

By Taxi/Rideshare: A taxi from Manhattan to Staten Island can cost anywhere from $25–$50, depending on the area and traffic.

Cost:

Staten Island Ferry: Free.

Staten Island Greenbelt: Free to explore.

Richmond Town: Admission to the historic village is around $10.

Staten Island Museum: Tickets are approximately $8–$10 for adults.

National Lighthouse Museum: Admission is around $7.

The boroughs of Queens, Bronx, and Staten Island each have unique cultural and historical offerings that provide a deeper look into New York City beyond the typical tourist hotspots. Whether you're visiting the lush green spaces and art museums of Queens, exploring the iconic sports and cultural landmarks of the Bronx, or taking in the views and history of Staten Island, these neighbourhoods promise enriching experiences. Getting to each is easy via public transit, and the costs are generally affordable, making them great options for visitors looking to expand their New York City adventure.

Chapter 7. Where to stay?

Luxury Hotels

The Plaza Hotel

What to Expect: The Plaza Hotel is one of New York City's most well-known and magnificent hotels, offering an unparalleled blend of historic grandeur and modern comforts. Its magnificent Beaux-Arts design has made it a symbol of grandeur for more than a century. Guests may expect excellent service, big apartments, and lavish public spaces. The hotel boasts:

• Our Classic Rooms and Suites have exquisite furnishings, marble bathtubs, and premium amenities.

• The Palm Court, the hotel's renowned dining spot, offers afternoon tea in a sumptuous setting.

• The Plaza Food Hall provides a variety of gourmet dining options.

• The Plaza Spa offers luxurious treatments for relaxation and regeneration.

• VIP Services include butlers, chauffeurs, and tailored concierge services to fulfil all requirements.

How to Get There:

The N, Q, R and W trains all stop at the 57th Street - 7th Avenue station, making the hotel conveniently accessible by tube.

The hotel's prime position in Manhattan provides convenient access to taxis and ridesharing services near major attractions.

• Buses (M5, M6, and M7) stop near the hotel on 5th Avenue.

• The Plaza Hotel is ideally located near Central Park, Times Square, and Broadway.

Cost:

• Room rates: Standard rooms begin at $1,000 per night, while suites vary from $2,500 to $6,000 per night according to extras.

• The Palm Court charges $50 to $100 per person for afternoon tea. Fine dining at other hotel restaurants might cost more than $100 per person.

The St. Regis New York

What to Expect: The St. Regis New York offers timeless luxury in the heart of Midtown Manhattan. With a rich history dating back to 1904, this hotel combines old-world beauty with modern comfort. Guests may experience a regal atmosphere and top-tier services, including:

• Luxurious rooms and suites with exquisite furnishings, linens, and sophisticated decor, some with views of the metropolitan cityscape.

King Cole Bar, famed for its trademark Bloody Mary cocktail, offers an elegant setting for evening drinks.

• Astor Court, the hotel's fine-dining restaurant, serves modern American cuisine in a stylish environment.

• Exclusive Butler Service: Personalised service for a memorable stay.

• The St. Regis Spa provides luxurious treatments to relax and unwind in style.

How to Get There:

Subway: The hotel is located at 2 East 55th Street and 5th Avenue. The nearest tube stations are 5th Avenue/53rd Street (E and M lines) and 57th Street/Seventh Avenue (N, Q, R and W trains).

• Easily accessible by taxi or rideshare from anywhere in Manhattan. The hotel is centrally located, thus travel time varies depending on your location.

• Several bus lines (M1, M2, and M3) stop near the hotel on 5th Avenue.

The St. Regis Hotel is ideally positioned near Central Park, Times Square, and the Museum of Modern Art.

Cost:

Standard rooms at the St. Regis New York start at $800 per night, while suites range from $2,000 to $10,000 a night, depending on size and exclusivity.

Lunch at Astor Court costs $50-150 per person, while beverages at King Cole Bar cost $20-$30.

Both hotels provide excellent experiences, making them ideal for tourists looking for a luxurious stay in the heart of New York City.

Budget-Friendly Options

Hotel 31

What to Expect: Hotel 31 is affordable in Manhattan's Kips Bay district. The hotel's basic and reasonably priced rooms are ideal for tourists who prioritise value over luxury while yet seeking a nice, clean place to stay in a handy location.

• Hotel 31 provides modest rooms with standard amenities including comfortable beds, cable TV, free Wi-Fi, and shared or private bathrooms. Some rooms feature private bathrooms, while others share facilities with other visitors.

The hotel prioritises clean and safe accommodations above needless frills. It's great for individuals who like a low-key experience yet value the convenience of staying in Manhattan.

• The Kips Bay area is tranquil and residential, with nearby cafés, restaurants, and shopping. The Empire State Building, Madison Square Garden, and Times Square are all within easy walking distance.

How to Get There:

Underground: Hotel 31 is located at 120 East 31st Street. The closest tube station is 33rd Street (4, 6 trains), which is just a short walk away. The R and W trains at 28th Street are also nearby.

• Taxi/Rideshare: A 30-minute ride from LaGuardia Airport and 45 minutes from JFK Airport. Expect a fare of $30-$50.

• Bus routes M1, M2, and M3 stop near the hotel on Park Avenue South and Lexington Avenue.

The hotel is within walking distance of Madison Square Garden, Times Square, and the Flatiron Building.

Cost:

Hotel 31 offers standard rooms ranging from $100 to $150 a night, based on season and room type. Private bathroom rooms cost more than shared bathroom accommodations.

The Bowery House

What to Expect: Located on Manhattan's Lower East Side, the Bowery House is a stylish but affordable option. This ancient hotel provides a mix of private and shared dorm-style rooms. It's ideal for budget-conscious tourists who desire a blend of history and modern comfort.

• Stylish, Minimalist Rooms: The hotel offers both shared and private rooms with sleek, minimalist designs. The shared rooms are bunk-style, whilst private rooms provide more space and comfort at a little higher fee.

The Bowery House's relaxed and innovative environment caters to a younger demographic. The hotel has a pleasant lounge area where guests may interact, relax, or work. The rooftop offers spectacular views of the city.

• The Lower East Side is known for its vibrant nightlife, trendy stores, and diverse food choices. The Bowery House is a short walk from SoHo, Chinatown, and Little Italy, making it easy to explore these lively districts.

How to Get There:

The hotel's nearest tube stations are Bowery (J, Z lines) and 2nd Avenue (F trains), both a 5-minute walk away.

• Cab/Rideshare: A 25-minute travel from LaGuardia Airport costs $25-$40. The travel from JFK Airport takes around 40 minutes and costs between $50 and $70.

• The M15 bus stops nearby on Bowery Street, making it a handy option for those going by bus.

The hotel is perfectly positioned near the East River, Chinatown, and SoHo, giving guests quick access to the vibrant Lower East Side district.

Cost:

The Bowery House has shared rooms beginning from $60-$100 per night and private rooms ranging from $130-$200 per night, depending on season and availability.

Both hotels provide cheap rooms with easy access to Manhattan's top attractions, making them good choices for anyone looking to explore the city without breaking the bank.

Unique Accommodations

The New York Edition

What to Expect: The New York Edition is a magnificent boutique hotel located in Manhattan's historic Flatiron District, blending modern flare with traditional elegance. Located in the historic MetLife Building, it offers contemporary accommodations with a focus on simplicity and comfort.

• The New York Edition has contemporary rooms and suites with floor-to-ceiling windows for stunning city views. Many accommodations provide lavish amenities like soft mattresses, big bathrooms with deep soaking tubs, and stylish décor.

• The Edition Hotel restaurant serves unique and fresh dishes. The Lobby Bar is a posh spot for cocktails, while the Bar Room is a refined setting for casual meals.

The hotel has a contemporary fitness facility, wellness facilities, and a rooftop bar with breathtaking views of the city skyline.

• The hotel's concierge team provides personalised service, such as organising theatrical tickets and special excursions.

How to Get There:

Underground: The New York Edition is located at 5 Madison Avenue. The nearest tube stations are 23rd Street (N, Q, R, and W trains) and 28th Street (one line), both of which are a short walk away.

• Taxi/Rideshare: The travel from LaGuardia to JFK Airport takes around 30 and 45 minutes, respectively.

Public transport: The hotel is easily accessible by the M1, M2, and M3 buses that go along Madison Avenue.

The hotel's position in the Flatiron District provides convenient access to major landmarks such as Madison Square Park, Union Square, and the Empire State Building.

Cost:

The New York Edition's standard rooms cost between $700 and $900 per night. Larger suites or rooms with views of the Empire State Building might cost between $1,500 and $3,000 per night, depending on the season.

The Hotel Chelsea

What to Expect: The Hotel Chelsea is a historic hotel in Manhattan's Chelsea area with a long history and cultural culture. It has long been recognised for hosting artists, musicians, and writers, and it today offers a unique and eclectic stay that blends traditional grandeur with modern amenities.

The Hotel Chelsea is known for its distinctive, bohemian vibe. The hotel has a range of lodging options, including basic rooms, suites, and loft apartments. Each room is distinctively designed, with antique furniture, unusual décor, and artwork that represents the hotel's rich history.

• The hotel has a significant creative past, with some rooms displaying artwork from visiting artists. It has been home to notable personalities such as Bob Dylan, Patti Smith, and Sid Vicious, giving it a distinct cultural identity.

• Hotel amenities include complimentary Wi-Fi, a fitness centre, and a library. It also has a cosy bar where tourists may unwind.

• As a cultural landmark, the hotel hosts art exhibits and events, creating a unique and engaging experience for guests.

How to Get There:

Underground: The Hotel Chelsea is located at 222 West 23rd Street. The closest tube stations are 23rd Street (C and E trains) and 28th Street (1 train), both of which are within walking distance.

• Taxi/rideshare: About 30 minutes from LaGuardia Airport and 45 minutes from JFK Airport.

• Buses, including M5 and M7, stop near 7th and 6th Avenue.

The hotel's central position provides travellers with a quick walk to Madison Square Garden, Times Square, and the High Line.

Cost:

Hotel Chelsea offers hotel prices ranging from $250-$400 per night for conventional rooms to $500-$1000 per night for suites and lofts, according to size and style.

Both hotels provide unique experiences, with The New York Edition providing a modern, sophisticated stay and The Hotel Chelsea having a more eclectic, historic appeal, making them ideal for visitors looking for one-of-a-kind accommodations in New York City.

Chapter 8. Cooking and Dining Experiences

Bagels, pizza, and hot dogs are classic New York City cuisine.

Bagels, pizza, and hot dogs are classic New York City cuisine.

New York City is well-known for its delectable food, and no vacation to the Big Apple is complete without sampling some of its classic gastronomic favourites. Bagels, pizza, and hot dogs are among the most popular, each with its history and taste that has become an essential part of the city's culture.

Bagels

Overview: The thick, chewy texture of the New York bagel distinguishes it from other bagels across the globe. It is often boiled before baking, giving it its distinctive crispy exterior and soft inside. Bagels are often served with cream cheese and customary toppings like lox (smoked salmon), onions, and capers. Some of the most popular bagel varieties in NYC are everything, sesame, plain, and poppy seed.

Where to Get Them:

• Russ & Daughters (179 E Houston St) is a New York institution that serves superb bagels with lox and cream cheese.

• Ess-a-Bagel (831 3rd Ave) offers enormous, freshly cooked bagels with customised toppings.

Absolute Bagels (2788 Broadway) on the Upper West Side serves delicious bagels with a variety of toppings.

Cost:

• Plain bagels often cost $1-$2 each.

Bagel sandwiches with cream cheese and smoked salmon may cost $5 to $10, depending on the ingredients.

Pizza

Overview: New York-style pizza is defined by its large, thin, and foldable slices. The pizza features a crispy yet chewy crust and is often topped with basic components including tomato sauce, mozzarella cheese and a range of toppings such as pepperoni, sausage and vegetables. A proper New York slice has a high cheese-to-crust ratio and can be folded in half without falling apart.

The Margherita pizza is a classic, although there are several variations, including the white pizza (no tomato sauce) and the Sicilian (a square-shaped, thicker crust pizza).

Where to Get It:

• Joe's Pizza (7 Carmine St) has been providing authentic New York-style pizza since 1975 and is a popular choice among locals and tourists.

• Di Fara Pizza (1424 Avenue J, Brooklyn) is a top pizza spot in the city, serving fresh ingredients and handcrafted pies.

• Lombardi's Pizza (32 Spring St) claims to be America's first pizzeria, serving real wood-fired pizza since 1905.

Cost:

• Pizza prices vary by location, ranging from $3 to $5 per piece.

• Pizzas range from $12 to $30 based on size and toppings.

Hot dogs

Overview: The New York hot dog is a must-try street food known for its distinct flavour and long history in the city. Hot dogs in New York are often served on a soft bun with mustard, ketchup, sauerkraut, and onions. They are often prepared with a combination of beef and pork, yielding a savoury and moist flavour. A New York hot dog has a special place in the city's culinary landscape, whether eaten from a street cart or at a well-known hot dog stand.

Where to Get Them:

Gray's Papaya (2090 Broadway) offers the Recession Special, which includes two hot dogs and a drink for $5. It's a classic, no-frills location.

• Nathan's Famous (1310 Surf Ave, Coney Island) is the most well-known hot dog eatery in NYC, especially for its annual hot dog eating competition.

• Papaya King (179 E 86th St) serves delicious hot dogs paired with tropical fruit drinks.

Cost:

• Hot dogs from street vendors often cost $2-3.

• Gray's Papaya serves hot dog combo dinners with drinks for $5-$7.

• Nathan's Famous hot dogs cost $4 to $6 per dog, depending on size and toppings.

• Popular foods in New York City include bagels, pizza, and hot dogs. Whether you're buying a fast bagel in the morning, enjoying a slice of pizza while roaming around, or eating a hot dog from a street cart, these meals deliver a true NYC experience.

• These dishes are widely accessible in the city, from street vendors to renowned restaurants, and affordable to all budgets. Prices for street food range from $2 to $3, but a full meal in a restaurant or pizza shop costs between $10 and $30.

When visiting New York City, these classic meals are a great and economical way to experience the city's rich culinary heritage.

Best restaurants and cafes.

Resturanrsnts

Eleven Madison Park

What to Expect: Eleven Madison Park is a world-renowned fine dining restaurant situated in the heart of Manhattan, known for its innovative and creative approach to modern American cuisine. With a focus on seasonal ingredients, the restaurant offers a tasting menu that is constantly changed to reflect the best cuisine and techniques available. The experience is on both creativity and flavour, with each meal presented as a visual and gourmet masterpiece.

Eleven Madison Park holds three Michelin stars, a James Beard Award, and was ranked one of the world's best restaurants by The World's 50 Best Restaurants.

• The tasting menu features savoury and sweet options, including vegetarian, seafood, and plant-based options.

The restaurant's stunning art-deco building offers a luxurious and relaxing atmosphere. With simple furniture and huge windows overlooking Madison Square Park, the interior design contributes to a wonderful dining experience.

• Expect great, individualised service. The waitstaff is well-educated and knowledgeable, often providing details on the ingredients, cooking techniques, and presentation of each dish.

How to Get There:

Subway: Eleven Madison Park is located at 11 Madison Avenue. The closest tube stations are 23rd Street (N, Q, R, W trains) and 28th Street (one line), all of which are a short walk away.

• Taxi/Rideshare: 30 minutes from LaGuardia Airport, 45 minutes from JFK Airport.

• Madison Avenue is readily accessible from many parts of the city by bus routes M1, M2, and M23.

Cost:

The sample supper at Eleven Madison Park costs around $335 per person. Wine pairings are available for an additional $195-$300.

• Optional add-ons, including special food or exclusive activities, may have extra prices. Reservations are highly recommended, especially on important occasions.

Le Bernardin

What to Expect: Le Bernardin is a Michelin-starred French seafood restaurant that offers an elevated dining experience focused on exceptional seafood dishes. Eric Ripert founded Le Bernardin, which is renowned for its exceptional quality and elegance. The restaurant's dishes mix classic French techniques with fresh, sustainable seafood imported from across the world.

Le Bernardin has three Michelin stars and is consistently ranked as one of the world's best restaurants. It also has the James Beard Award for Outstanding Service.

Le Bernardin's menu offers both a la carte and tasting options. Signature dishes include Tuna Tartare, Poached Lobster, and Black Bass, all made with seasonal ingredients. Vegetarian options are available upon request, however seafood remains the primary focus.

• The dining room is elegant with soft lighting, polished wood, and modern art pieces. The environment is classy but pleasant, making it great for a variety of special occasions or a luxurious night out.

• Le Bernardin provides exceptional service, paying attention to every detail, including dinner presentations and wine pairings. Expect attentive and knowledgeable staff to enhance your dining experience with individual attention.

How to Get There:

Subway: Le Bernardin is located at 155 W 51st St. Nearby subway stations are 47th-50th Streets-Rockefeller Centre (B, D, F, M lines) and 49th Street (N, Q, R, W trains), all within walking distance.

• Taxi/Rideshare: It takes around 25 minutes from LaGuardia Airport and 40 minutes from JFK.

Public transit alternatives include the M5, M7, and M20 buses that stop on 7th Avenue, as well as the M104 on 51st Street.

Cost:

• The prix fixe lunch menu is $65-$85 per person, while the chef's tasting menu costs $125-175 per person.

• Wine pairings range from $85 to $200, depending on the selection and number of courses.

• A la Carte: Dishes vary from $30 to $60, depending on ingredients and preparation.

Both Eleven Madison Park and Le Bernardin provide incredible fine dining experiences with great service and world-class cuisine; however, Eleven Madison Park is more daring with contemporary American cuisine, whilst Le Bernardin showcases the finest of French seafood gastronomy.

Cafe

Russ & Daughters Cafe

What to Expect: Russ & Daughters Cafe is a New York City institution known for serving classic Jewish deli food with a modern twist. Established in 1914, it's a favourite location for anybody searching for traditional New York tastes, particularly those associated with smoked salmon, bagels, and Jewish comfort foods. The café, situated on the Lower East Side, is a more casual extension of the original Russ & Daughters Appetisers, which has been a New York culinary institution for over a century.

The menu includes bagels with lox and cream cheese, matzo ball soup, knishes, and smoked fish platters. Fan favourites include latkes (potato pancakes) and bagels with sable, which come with a range of smoked fish options.

• The space combines the feel of a historic deli with the elegance of a contemporary café. Its warm, bright atmosphere makes it perfect for a casual meal or breakfast with friends or family.

• Service: Expect knowledgeable and friendly staff to help you through the menu, propose pairings, and provide recommendations for first-time customers.

How to Get There:

Underground: Russ & Daughters Cafe is located at 127 Orchard Street. The closest tube stations are Delancey Street (F, M trains) and Essex Street (J, Z trains), all of which are within walking distance.

• Taxi/Rideshare: Travel time is about 25 minutes from LaGuardia Airport and 40 minutes from JFK Airport.

Public transport: The M9 and M14D buses stop nearby, making Orchard Street conveniently accessible.

Cost:

• Depending on the kind of fish, bagels with lox and cream cheese go from $8 to $15.

• Latkes and other deli staples go from $10 to $20 per dish.

• Full meals or platters range from $20 to $40, depending on the selections.

• The café's brunch menu includes bagels, smoked salmon and spreads priced between $15 and $25 per person.

Dominique Ansel Bakery

What to Expect: Dominique Ansel Bakery is a New York City institution known for its creative pastries, including the world-renowned Cronut®. Dominique Ansel, a French pastry chef, established the bakery, which has redefined modern pastries by putting creative spins on traditional French and American baked goods. The space is elegant and simple, with a warm, welcoming atmosphere in which visitors may enjoy both classic and new sweets.

• Menu Highlights: In addition to the Cronut®, the menu includes cookies, tarts, eclairs, and seasonal treats. The bakery is known for blending traditional favourites with novel ingredients and procedures, such as the frozen s'more (a funny take on the campfire treat) and the kitchen sink cookie (which has everything from chocolate chips to pretzels).

• The bakery's design is clean and modern, with large windows allowing for natural light. It's a warm atmosphere that encourages customers to remain and enjoy their purchases, whether at one of the few tables or standing at the bar.

• Service: Expect friendly and knowledgeable staff to help you navigate the menu, particularly if you're unfamiliar with popular items like Cronut®.

How to Get There:

Dominique Ansel Bakery is located at 189 Spring Street in SoHo and is easily accessible by tube. Spring Street (C, E trains) and Prince Street (N, Q, R, W trains) are the nearest tube stations and are both a short walk away.

The bakery is about 30 minutes from LaGuardia Airport and 45 minutes from JFK Airport via taxi or rideshare.

• By Bus: The bakery is readily accessible by the M20 and M5 buses that pass near Spring Street.

Cost:

• Cronuts® normally costs $6-$7 per serving, although prices may vary depending on the flavour of the month.

• Pastries including cookies, tarts, and eclairs often cost $3-7 each.

• Pastries and speciality delicacies, such as frozen s'mores or seasonal tarts, may cost between $8-15.

Russ & Daughters Cafe and Dominique Ansel Bakery provide diverse culinary experiences in New York City. Russ & Daughters evokes New York's Jewish deli tradition, while Dominique Ansel Bakery takes pastry innovation to new heights with vibrant, inventive designs. Whether you're craving a savoury bagel with lox or a sweet, delicious Cronut®, these are must-stops on your holiday.

Food Trucks and Street Food

Red Hook Lobster Pound

What to Expect: Red Hook Lobster Pound is a renowned food truck that sells Maine lobster rolls on the streets of New York City. This food truck is famous for serving some of the city's freshest and most flavourful lobster rolls, as well as a variety of lobster-based dishes inspired by New England fishing shacks. Whether you're looking for a typical lobster roll, lobster soup, or lobster mac and cheese, Red Hook Lobster Pound offers an authentic and delectable seafood-eating experience.

• The Maine Lobster bun is the menu's centrepiece, featuring generous amounts of lobster meat on a toasted and buttery bun. Other popular choices include lobster grilled cheese, lobster soup, and lobster tacos. They also serve clam chowder and sometimes provide seasonal specials.

The Red Hook Lobster Pound is a food truck with a casual, street-style vibe and delicious meals. It's excellent for those on the go looking for a quick yet satisfying seafood dinner. They often set up shop in various sections of the city, most notably in Brooklyn and Manhattan, so follow them on social media for the most up-to-date information.

• Service: Receive timely, pleasant service from competent staff who may provide ideas and explain menu alternatives.

How to Get There:

Subway food trucks are often seen in Brooklyn's DUMBO and Manhattan's FiDi. For DUMBO, take the F train to York Street; for FiDi, take the 2, 4, 5, J, or Z trains to Broad Street.

• Taxi/Rideshare: The truck's location may change, but apps like Uber or Lyft may assist you get close to the current stop.

• Bus routes B25 and B61 serve Red Hook and DUMBO.

Cost:

• Maine Lobster Roll costs around $22-$25.

• Lobster Grilled Cheese costs around $15-17.

• Lobster tacos often cost $6-$9 per.

• Lobster bisque costs about $7-$10.

Schmackary's (Cookies)

What to Expect: Schmackary's is a well-known cookie bakery famed for its wonderful, freshly baked cookies, which have become a must-try delicacy among New York City visitors. The bakery is well-known for its diverse selection of innovative and classic cookie varieties, all made with high-quality ingredients. Schmackary's is especially popular among those with a sweet tooth, delivering soft, chewy cookies that are bursting with taste in every bite.

• Menu Highlights: Schmackary's offers a range of cookie varieties such as Chocolate Chip, S'mores, Confetti, Red Velvet, and Cornflake Marshmallow. They also provide cookie cakes, sundaes, and milkshakes. Vegan and gluten-free options are available, so everyone may enjoy a treat.

• The bakery offers a welcoming and comfortable atmosphere. The vibrant design and delightful aroma of freshly baked cookies fill the air, making it the perfect spot for a sweet treat.

• Expect timely and friendly service. The staff is always happy to explain the cookies and help you choose the perfect treat.

How to Get There:

• Subway: Schmackary's is located at 59 W 45th St. The closest subway stations are Times Square-42nd Street (1, 2, 3, 7, N, Q, R, W, S) and 42nd Street-Bryant Park (B, D, F, M), all within a short walk from the bakery.

• Taxi/Rideshare: Travel time from LaGuardia Airport is roughly 25 minutes, while from JFK Airport is about 40 minutes.

• Schmackary's is conveniently accessible by bus from the M7, M42, and M104 lines.

Cost:

• Standard Cookies: Prices range from $2.50 to $4 per cookie, depending on size and taste.

- Cookie cakes range from $28 to $50, depending on size.

- Cookie sundaes usually cost $7-10.

- Milkshakes cost about $5-$7.

Whether you want a delicious lobster roll or a gourmet cookie, Red Hook Lobster Pound and Schmackary's provide some of the best street food experiences in New York City. These food trucks and bakeries are perfect for quick bites or luxurious treats, enabling you to experience the city's vibrant culinary culture while on the go.

Chapter 9: Shopping in the City

High-end boutiques

High-end boutiques in New York City.

New York is well-known for its luxury shopping, with high-end shops providing an exclusive and tailored shopping experience that reflects the city's standing as a worldwide fashion powerhouse. Whether you're seeking classic luxury or the most cutting-edge designs, NYC's high-end boutiques cater to a broad range of preferences, guaranteeing that discriminating shoppers may discover something unique and outstanding.

Here's a look at some of the best high-end shops to visit:

Chanel

What To Expect: Chanel represents the pinnacle of luxury, with high-quality, timeless designs. Their store sells everything from Chanel's trademark tweed coats, quilted purses, classic suits, and high-fashion shoes to unique fragrances and accessories. Every piece reflects the brand's characteristic elegant and sophisticated Coco Chanel look.

Notable features include personalised customer service, limited-edition collections, and unique products.

How to get there: Chanel's main shop is on 57th Street and Madison Avenue, near Central Park. The 57th Street station is conveniently accessible by tube, with the F, N, Q, R and W lines.

Cost: Prices for products like the Chanel Classic Flap Bag begin at about $5,000, while ready-to-wear clothes vary from $1,500 to $15,000.

Gucci

What To Expect: Gucci is recognised for its high-end leather products, designer clothes, and distinctive accessories. Their shop combines bold designs, imaginative aesthetics, and grandeur, offering everything from iconic GG logo belts to high-end handbags and ready-to-wear collections for men and women. The store often includes products from limited collections and collaborations, offering a special shopping experience for people looking for unique goods.

Notable features include a mix of traditional and modern styles, a diverse assortment of shoes, bags, and accessories, and in-store events for personalised shopping.

How to Get There: Gucci's main shop is at 375 West Broadway, in the SoHo neighbourhood, a fashionable neighbourhood famed for its artistic ambience. Spring Street station is accessible by tube using the C and E lines.

A Gucci purse may cost between $1,000 and $4,000, while ready-to-wear pieces run from $500 to $5,000, depending on the piece.

Louis Vuitton

What to Expect: Louis Vuitton is a premium brand renowned for its monogrammed bags, fashion-forward clothes, and trademark accessories. The company is well-known for its robust workmanship, which makes goods like the LV Speedy bag and Neverfull bags coveted. The shop also has limited edition collections and collaborations, guaranteeing that you have a completely unique experience.

Notable features include classic leather goods, high-fashion garments and accessories, and exclusive seasonal collections.

How to Get There: Louis Vuitton's main shop is at 1 East 57th Street, near Fifth Avenue. It's a short walk from Central Park and readily accessible from the E, F, N, Q, and R lines at 57th Street Station.

Louis Vuitton monogram bags vary in price from $1,200 to $5,000, while apparel items may cost between $500 and $4,000.

Tiffany & Co. offers exquisite jewellery with timeless elegance. Whether you are seeking engagement rings, diamonds or elegant cutlery, the boutique has a wide selection of attractive, high-end goods. The brand's iconic blue boxes and beautiful designs are in great demand for both special occasions and daily luxury.

Notable features include an exquisite assortment of diamonds, gold jewellery, and vintage designs, as well as custom-designed jewellery possibilities for a genuinely personalised experience. The ambience is elegant and pleasant, and the staff is informed.

How to Get There: Tiffany & Co.'s main shop is at 727 Fifth Avenue, just across from Central Park. The underground station at 59th Street is accessible by the N, Q, R and W lines.

Tiffany jewellery prices start at $300, with engagement rings ranging from $5,000 to $50,000 or more depending on the design and diamond.

Prada

What to Expect: Prada is the epitome of high-fashion refinement, famed for its crisp designs, sumptuous materials, and daring styling choices. The store sells a variety of leather purses, fitted suits, and striking shoes, as well as sunglasses, scarves, and jewellery. Prada offers a one-of-a-kind shopping experience by combining historical craftsmanship with current styles.

Notable features include signature Prada nylon bags and leather accessories, high-fashion collections with innovative and stylish designs, and a modern, clean appearance that reflects the brand's cutting-edge creations.

How to Get There: The Prada store is situated at 575 Broadway in SoHo, which is home to many other high-end businesses. The Prince Street station is accessible by the tube (N, Q, R and W lines).

Prada purses start at about $1,500, while ready-to-wear goods range between $600 and $4,000.

Fendi

What to Expect: Fendi is another Italian luxury company renowned for its lavish fur designs, leather purses, and high-fashion clothing. The store sells a broad range of distinctive items, including the renowned Baguette bag, as well as men's and women's clothes, footwear, and accessories. Fendi often showcases fashion-forward collections, providing a luxurious shopping experience.

Notable features include unique goods such as Fendi furs and statement bags, as well as high-fashion clothes and accessories with a focus on luxury. Additionally, personalised services are available for bespoke pieces and exclusive collections.

How to Get There: Fendi's main shop is situated at 51 East 57th Street, near Fifth Avenue. Easily accessible by tube at 57th Street station (N, Q, R, W, S lines).

Fendi bags may cost anywhere from $1,500 to $6,000. Clothing items normally cost between $500 and $4,000.

High-end stores in New York City provide incomparable luxury and elegance for individuals seeking rare designer clothes. NYC's luxury retail culture is second to none, with iconic names like Chanel and Louis Vuitton alongside modern labels like Prada and Fendi. Whether you're looking for classic items or the newest trends, these shops provide an unforgettable shopping experience that reflects the city's role as a worldwide fashion powerhouse.

Local markets and thrift stores

Local Markets and Thrift Stores in New York City

New York City is not simply a luxury shopping destination, but also a thriving centre for individuals looking for unusual, one-of-a-kind things. Whether you're looking for antique treasures, artisanal goods, or local crafts, the city's local markets and thrift stores provide a diverse selection of items that you won't find anywhere. These shops provide a more personalised, cheap shopping experience and are ideal for people wishing to discover the city's culture via its distinctive offers. Here's a deeper look at New York City's top neighbourhood markets and secondhand stores.

Chelsea Market

What To Expect:

Chelsea Market is an indoor marketplace that sells artisanal cuisine, fashion products, and handcrafted crafts. Originally the headquarters of the National Biscuit Company (Nabisco), the market today has a broad range of local sellers offering anything from gourmet cuisine and fresh vegetables to vintage apparel and artisan jewellery. It's an excellent site to explore the mix of NYC's current culinary and retail culture.

• Shoppers may expect to discover vintage apparel, homemade soaps, local art, and handcrafted leather products.

• Chelsea Market is recognised for its gourmet food sellers, including Lobster Place (seafood), Los Tacos No. 1, and Sarabeth's.

• The market's industrial-chic design has exposed brick walls, art deco details, and a cosy ambience, ideal for a leisurely walk.

How to get there:

Chelsea Market is situated at 75 Ninth Avenue, between 15th and 16th streets. The A, C, and E lines stop at the 14th Street station, while the L train takes you to 8th Avenue.

Cost: Prices vary greatly based on the item purchased. Food and small artisan things may cost $5 to $30, and antique and handmade goods may cost $10 to $100 or more.

Brooklyn Flea

What To Expect:

The Brooklyn Flea is one of NYC's most popular flea markets, with a wide selection of vintage apparel, antiques, upcycled furniture, handcrafted products, and local art. It's a great place for cheap shoppers searching for eccentric, one-of-a-kind products with a historical twist. During various seasons, the market has sites in DUMBO and Fort Greene, and it's one of the city's most diverse shopping destinations.

• Shop for vintage clothes, vinyl records, repurposed furniture, handcrafted jewellery, and art by local craftsmen.

• Food: The market offers local and foreign cuisine, including craft beer and baked products.

• The Brooklyn Flea offers a laid-back, hipster ambience ideal for thrifting and collecting.

How to get there:

The DUMBO site is at 80 Pearl Street. To get there via tube, take the F train to York Street. The Fort Greene site is accessible by riding the C train to the Washington Avenue stop.

Prices at Brooklyn Flea vary from $5 for little items to $100+ for antique furniture and high-end jewellery.

The Market NYC

The Market NYC is a unique indoor and outdoor market in the East Village that sells locally manufactured apparel, accessories, home décor, and art. Unlike typical flea markets, The Market offers a tailored experience with a mix of new designers, local artisans, and emerging brands.

• Shopping options include local art, handcrafted jewellery, vintage apparel, boho-chic accessories, and unique home décor goods.

• The market has a fashionable, artistic vibe with vibrant colours, unusual designs, and an open-air layout for a pleasant, community-centric shopping experience.

The Market NYC is situated at 129-131 2nd Avenue, between 8th and 9th Streets, in the East Village. It is readily accessible by tube, with the L line on 1st Avenue and the N, Q, R and W trains at 8th Street station.

Cost: Accessories and jewellery range from $10 to $50, while home décor and apparel cost $50 to $200.

Housing Works Thrift Stores

Housing Works runs thrift stores in NYC, offering donated designer items, antique treasures, and second-hand furniture. All revenues from these businesses benefit their aim to battle homelessness and

AIDS in New York City. This allows you to buy not just for unique, high-quality things, but also to contribute back to the community.

Housing Works specialises in designer apparel, antique handbags, books, home furnishings, and art.

• The shops are well-organised and provide an upmarket, boutique-like thrifting experience. The range of things ensures that there is always something for everyone's taste and budget.

Housing Works has many sites in NYC, including SoHo's Crosby Street and Chelsea's 17th Street. It is readily accessible by tube, with the C and E trains stopping at West 4th Street and the L train stopping at 14th Street station.

Housing Works offers affordable designer apparel, with prices ranging from $50 to $200+. Books, home décor, and furnishings all range in price, with most goods ranging from $10 to $100.

Goodwill New York

Expect to find gently worn things at low costs at Goodwill NYC's several locations. While the shop is well-known for its low-cost items, it also has a great selection of vintage apparel, household products, and accessories. It's a great site for budget-conscious customers looking for deals.

• Shopping options include classic jeans, vintage knitwear, second-hand furniture, shoes, kitchenware, and books.

• The businesses are organised and well-maintained, with an old-school thrift-shop vibe that allows for a thrilling treasure search for discounts.

How to Get There: Goodwill stores are located across the city, including popular areas like Chelsea, Harlem, and Brooklyn. They are easily accessible by tube, with stops often along the 1, 2, 3, and A lines.

Goodwill provides inexpensive rates, beginning at $1-5 for modest goods like books or accessories. Clothes goods are normally priced between $5 to $25, with more costly things such as designer clothes costing more.

Local markets and thrift stores in New York City provide a varied and diverse shopping experience for everyone, from vintage enthusiasts to environmentally aware customers. Whether you're seeking designer deals, antique furnishings, or one-of-a-kind artisan items, these markets and stores provide a unique chance to bring something remarkable home. Best of all, these locations provide an opportunity to experience New York's local culture, community spirit, and ecological buying methods. So, if you're a knowledgeable shopper hunting for one-of-a-kind items, be sure to stop by these local gems on your next visit.

Chapter 10. Cultural and Historical Landmarks

Broadway & Performing Arts

Broadway and the Performing Arts in New York City

New York City is the world's cultural centre, and Broadway is its crown gem. Broadway, known as the epicentre of live theatre, has a centuries-long tradition of presenting the greatest and brightest performances. Beyond Broadway, New York City has a vibrant performing arts community that includes everything from contemporary dance performances and experimental theatre to opera, classical music, and ballet. The city's diverse performance offerings appeal to every taste, making it a popular destination for cultural enthusiasts from all over the globe.

Broadway: The Heart of Theatre.

Overview:

Broadway is more than simply a street in Manhattan; it is an internationally recognised area associated with world-class theatre. With nearly 40 theatres in and around Times Square, Broadway is the apex of American theatre. Broadway shows vary from musicals and dramas to comedies and revivals of classic works, with many including stars from both the stage and the cinema. Productions including "The Lion King," "Hamilton," "The Phantom of the Opera," and "Wicked" have become famous, with some lasting decades.

What To Expect:

• Broadway offers diverse performances, including musicals, classic plays, and experimental theatre.

Large-scale shows will include complex sets, costumes, and spectacular choreography.

Broadway musicals often include well-known performers, singers, and dancers, providing a remarkable experience for theatre aficionados.

How to get there:

Broadway theatres are situated in Manhattan's Theatre District, which is centred on Times Square. This region is readily accessible by tube, using the 1, 2, 3, 7, N, Q, R or W trains to Times Square-42nd Street station.

Cost:

Ticket costs for Broadway musicals range from $50 to $500, depending on the production and seating arrangement. For other affordable choices, visit the TKTS counter for reduced same-day tickets, which may be up to 50% off normal prices.

Off-Broadway: Intimate, Innovative Performances

Overview:

Off-Broadway theatres provide more intimate shows than its bigger Broadway counterparts, with seating for less than 500 people. These venues showcase a variety of experimental works, new plays, and avant-garde musicals. Off-Broadway performances often have a more experimental tone, giving a forum for new authors and cutting-edge plays.

What To Expect:

• Off-Broadway shows are noted for their innovative approach to narrative and acting.

• Smaller, more intimate venues: Fewer seats provide a more personal connection to the act.

• Off-Broadway theatres showcase rising stars and developing talent, providing an excellent opportunity to discover new performers.

How to get there:

Off-Broadway theatres are located across Manhattan, primarily in SoHo, Greenwich Village, and the East Village. Many of these locations are readily accessible by tube, with stops at 14th Street-Union Square, Astor Place, and West 4th Street.

Cost:

Off-Broadway plays often have lower ticket rates than Broadway, ranging between $20 to $150.

The Met Opera: A World-Class Experience.

Overview:

The Metropolitan Opera House at Lincoln Centre is among the most prominent opera venues in the world. It is home to the Metropolitan Opera Company, which performs some of the best operas with globally famous artists. The Met's vast, beautiful theatre and excellent acoustics provide opera enthusiasts with an immersive experience.

What To Expect:

• The Met invites great performers from throughout the world.

• Experience lavish shows with magnificent sets, extravagant costumes, and incredible performances.

• A diverse repertory of operas, including masterpieces by Verdi and Puccini as well as current works, caters to all tastes.

How to get there:

The Metropolitan Opera House is situated in Lincoln Centre on West 65th Street. The 1, 2, A, B, C, or D lines stop near Columbus Circle or 59th Street, making it conveniently accessible by underground.

Cost:

Ticket costs at the Met Opera vary from $50 to $400+, depending on the show and seating options.

New York City Ballet is the home of classical dance.

Overview:

The New York City Ballet (NYCB), based in Lincoln Centre, is one of the world's major ballet groups. The NYCB, known for its inventive choreographers and classical performances, delivers a diverse range of events, from the timeless beauty of Tchaikovsky's "The Nutcracker" to contemporary works by current choreographers. Whether you're a ballet fan or new to the art form, the NYCB provides a memorable experience.

What To Expect:

• World-class ballet dancers provide exquisite performances with passionate choreography.

• The NYCB presents a diverse range of works, including classic ballets and innovative contemporary ones.

• The David H. Koch Theatre at Lincoln Centre offers a breathtaking setting for ballet performances.

How to get there:

The David H. Koch Theatre is situated in Lincoln Centre. To reach Columbus Circle or 59th Street station, use the 1, 2, A, B, C, or D subway lines.

Cost:

Ticket costs typically vary from $25 and $150, with some luxury seats priced more.

Public Theatre: Experimental and Cutting-Edge Theatre

Overview:

The Public Theatre, located on Astor Place in Manhattan, is one of New York's most renowned experimental and avant-garde theatre organisations. Founded by Joseph Papp, it is committed to creating new works and pushing the frontiers of theatre. Some of the most well-known plays of the last few decades have opened at the Public Theatre, including "Hamilton" and "A Chorus Line."

What To Expect:

• The Public Theatre showcases innovative plays and musicals before they become popular.

• Socially relevant productions: Expect to witness work that addresses key topics and empowers under-represented populations.

• Intimate setting: The theatre provides a more intimate experience than bigger Broadway theatres, allowing for direct interaction between the audience and artists.

How to get there:

The Public Theatre is situated at 425 Lafayette Street. It is readily accessible by taking the N, Q, R, or W trains to 8th Street-New York University, or the 6 line to Astor Place.

Cost:

Ticket prices are often lower, ranging from $30 to $100 depending on the performance.

Jazz and Live Music Venues

Overview:

In addition to Broadway and ballet, New York City is well-known for its live music culture, especially jazz. The city's numerous historic jazz clubs, such as the Blue Note, Village Vanguard, and Birdland, provide compact spaces for world-class jazz performances. Whether you're a jazz fanatic or a casual listener, NYC offers a diverse range of live music experiences.

What To Expect:

• Experience high-quality live jazz music from renowned performers and developing talent.

• Small clubs provide a more intimate and personalised experience.

• NYC has many music scenes, including jazz, rock, hip-hop, classical, and indie.

How to get there:

Jazz clubs may be found across Manhattan, including popular locations in Greenwich Village, Midtown, and Harlem. They are readily accessible by tube.

Cost:

Jazz club tickets are normally priced between $20 to $50, with elite events costing more.

New York City's Broadway and performing arts sector provides an unrivalled cultural experience, whether you're seeing a blockbuster Broadway musical, seeing a cutting-edge Off-Broadway production, or enjoying a world-class ballet or opera. The variety of acts and locations guarantees that there is something for everyone, from casual theatregoers to die-hard arts enthusiasts. During your stay, immerse yourself in the city's thriving arts scene to experience the excitement and creativity that have helped to make New York the world's cultural capital.

Historical Sites: Ellis Island and 9/11 Memorial

New York City's historical sites include Ellis Island and the 9/11 Memorial.

New York City, with its rich and varied past, is home to numerous notable historical landmarks that have had a significant impact on both the country and the globe. Ellis Island and the 9/11 Memorial are notable examples of the country's complicated history of immigration, perseverance, and commemoration. These locations give unique insights into important times in American history, allowing visitors to contemplate their importance.

Ellis Island: Gateway to America.

Overview:

Ellis Island, situated in New York Harbour, is one of the United States' most historically important landmarks. It was the principal immigration point for millions of immigrants entering America throughout the late nineteenth and early twentieth centuries. From 1892 to 1954, about 12 million immigrants travelled through Ellis Island on their way to establish new lives in the United States. Today, the island houses the Ellis Island National Museum of Immigration, which chronicles the tales of these immigrants and their contributions to American civilisation.

What to see at Ellis Island:

The Ellis Island National Museum of Immigration is located in the rebuilt Main Building, which was previously the processing facility for immigrants. It features exhibits on the immigrant experience, the history of immigration in the United States, and the personal tales of people who passed through Ellis Island. The American Immigrant Wall of Honour, which displays the names of those who have passed through the island, and the Immigration History Room, where visitors can learn about the screening procedure that immigrants went through, are two of the most important exhibits.

• The Great Hall, formerly a busy centre for processing immigrants, has been painstakingly restored to offer a peek into the experience of people arriving in America.

The American Immigrant Wall of Honour recognises people and families who have contributed significantly to American culture, paying respect to the millions of immigrants who passed through Ellis Island.

• The Genealogy Centre allows visitors to follow their ancestors' trip through Ellis Island using digital archives, providing a useful experience for individuals interested in their family history.

How to get there:

Ellis Island is accessible by boat from Battery Park in Lower Manhattan or Liberty State Park in Jersey City. Statue Cruises operates ferries, and the voyage takes around 15-20 minutes. Visitors are advised to combine their visit to Ellis Island with a journey to the adjacent Statue of Liberty since the two are serviced by the same boat service.

Cost:

The cost of seeing Ellis Island is included with the Statue of Liberty ticket. As of 2024, the regular ticket to Ellis Island and the Statue of Liberty is $24 for adults, with discounts for children and seniors. Additional services, such as access to the Statue of Liberty's pedestal or crown, may result in increased ticket rates.

9/11 Memorial and Museum: A Tribute to Resiliency

Overview:

The 9/11 Memorial and Museum is located in the centre of Lower Manhattan, on the site of the old World Trade Centre complex, where the horrific September 11, 2001 attacks occurred. The monument and museum honour the approximately 3,000 people who died that day, as well as the resilience of New York City, the United States, and the rest of the globe. The monument includes two reflecting ponds where the original Twin Towers once stood, and the museum provides a thorough and emotive analysis of the events surrounding the catastrophe.

What to see at the 9/11 Memorial and Museum:

• The 9/11 Memorial Pools have two huge, square reflecting pools that represent the footprints of the twin buildings. The borders of the pools are etched with the names of everyone who perished in the assaults, forming a dramatic and moving monument. The soothing sound of cascading water contrasts with the hustle and bustle of the metropolis surrounding it.

• The 9/11 Museum provides a detailed and emotional experience of 9/11 and its aftermath. The exhibits feature images, artefacts, movies, and audio that depict the attacks, the lives lost, and the worldwide repercussions. The Twin Towers' original steel beams, a fire vehicle destroyed in the attacks, and personal tales of survival and courage are among the key displays. The museum's immersive displays invite visitors to ponder on the tragedy and its importance.

• The Survivor Tree, a Callery pear tree that survived the World Trade Centre collapse, represents perseverance. It was eventually cultivated and returned to the site, where it today flourishes as a living memorial to the resilience of those touched by the attacks.

• The Memorial Glade, a new addition to the 9/11 Memorial, honours individuals who died from diseases connected to the recovery activities. The glade commemorates the courage of first responders and recovery personnel who died as a result of linked health conditions.

How to get there:

The 9/11 Memorial and Museum is situated at 180 Greenwich Street, Lower Manhattan. The 1, 2, 4, 5, J, Z, and R lines all stop at nearby stations, including World Trade Centre, Cortlandt Street, and Fulton Street, making it conveniently accessible via underground. The PATH train from New Jersey also stops at the World Trade Centre Station, making it an accessible location for travellers from across the river.

Cost:

• The 9/11 Memorial is free and open every day from 7:30 AM to 9:00 PM.

• The 9/11 Museum charges an entrance fee of $26 per adult. Seniors, veterans, and children may get discounted admission, and tickets for special exhibits or guided tours can be purchased separately. The museum is open from 9:00 a.m. to 8:00 p.m., with extended hours on certain days.

Both Ellis Island and the 9/11 Memorial are strong and highly touching historical locations that allow visitors to reflect on pivotal times in American history. Ellis Island symbolises the ambitions and sufferings of millions of immigrants seeking a better life in the United States, while the 9/11 Memorial honours a nation's perseverance in the face of unspeakable tragedy. Visiting these locations gives a unique chance to grasp the problems and accomplishments that have defined New York City and the country, providing a remarkable experience for those who take the time to investigate their complex histories.

Chapter 11: Things to Do in NYC

Seasonal Activities & Events

4th of July Fireworks

What To Expect:

New York City's Fourth of July Fireworks display is one of the largest and most impressive Independence Day festivities in the nation. The major fireworks show is fired from many boats along the East River, illuminating the Manhattan skyline. Expect a spectacular, colourful extravaganza paired with music, with millions of people assembling in various spots across the city to watch.

Where and when?

• The fireworks may be watched from Brooklyn Bridge Park, Roosevelt Island, Pier 17 in the Seaport District, Long Island City in Queens, and Governors Island.

• The concert usually starts about 9:00 p.m. on July 4th.

How to get there:

Take the underground to neighbouring stations, such as Brooklyn Bridge Park (Brooklyn Heights) or Fulton Street (Manhattan), according to your viewing position.

• Consider taking a boat to Governors Island or Long Island City for stunning vistas.

• To guarantee a decent place, arrive early, particularly in busy areas like Brooklyn Bridge Park or Manhattan's Lower East Side.

Cost:

• Public viewing of fireworks is free, however, premium venues or activities, such as rooftop bars or dinner cruises, may have fees.

• Tickets for closer views on ferries and cruises normally cost between $50 and $150.

New York Film Festival

What To Expect:

The New York Film Festival (NYFF) is among the most prominent film festivals in the world. It presents a varied selection of foreign and American films, including world premieres, retrospectives, and special events with directors and actors. The festival provides a chance to witness cutting-edge film before it is distributed to the public.

Where and when?

• The principal venue is the Film Society of Lincoln Center's Walter Reade Theatre and Alice Tully Hall. Some events take happen at other Manhattan cinemas.

• When: The event normally lasts two weeks from late September to early October.

How to get there:

Subway: Take the 1, 2, 3, A, C, or E lines to 59th Street-Columbus Circle or Lincoln Centre.

• Several MTA bus routes operate through Lincoln Centre, including the M5, M7, M10, and M104.

Lincoln Centre, situated at 70 Lincoln Centre Plaza in Manhattan, is easily accessible by foot from surrounding neighbourhoods such as the Upper West Side.

Cost:

• Individual screening tickets vary from $15 to $50, depending on the movie and screening style (public admission, special events).

• Passes range from $300 to $1,000+ and include admission to several screenings and activities.

Halloween Parade & Pumpkin Flotilla

What To Expect:

The Halloween Parade and Pumpkin Flotilla is one of New York City's most enjoyable and distinctive Halloween celebrations. The Halloween Parade is a costume parade that travels through Greenwich Village, including elaborate costumes, floats, and entertainment. The Pumpkin Flotilla, which is often hosted in Central Park's Conservatory Water, is a joyful event in which families carve pumpkins, float them on the water, and watch them light up at nightfall.

Where and when?

• Halloween Parade:

• Location: Greenwich Village (6th Avenue between Spring and 16th Streets).

• When: October 31st, 7:00 PM to late at night.

• Pumpkin Flotilla:

• Location: Conservatory Water in Central Park (around 72nd Street).

• When: The Pumpkin Flotilla occurs in late October, often the weekend before Halloween.

How to get there:

• Halloween Parade:

To reach the parade route by tube, take the A, B, C, D, E, F or M lines to West 4th Street or Houston Street.

The M8 bus also passes through Greenwich Village.

• Pumpkin Flotilla:

• Take the Q, B, or C trains to 59th Street-Columbus Circle, then walk to the park.

Central Park is readily accessible by strolling from nearby neighbourhoods, including the Upper West Side and Midtown Manhattan.

Cost:

• While the Halloween Parade is free to watch, private parties and viewing spots may charge a fee.

• The Pumpkin Flotilla is free, however, some places may charge a nominal fee to carve a pumpkin (about $10-$20).

Easter Parade & Bonnet Festival

What To Expect:

The Easter Parade and Bonnet Festival is a joyful and unique event in which New Yorkers gather to celebrate Easter in style by displaying their most lavish and imaginative Easter bonnets. The event is not a parade in the classic sense, but rather a casual promenade along Fifth Avenue from 57th to 49th streets. Spectators may admire the colourful and innovative hats worn by the contestants, many of which are intricate and hilarious.

Where and when?

The procession will take place on Fifth Avenue between 57th and 49th Streets.

• When: The celebration takes place on Easter Sunday, often in April, from 10:00 AM to 4:00 PM.

How to get there:

Subway: N, Q, R, W, F, or M trains stop at Fifth Avenue/59th Street or Grand Central Station nearby.

• Walking: Fifth Avenue is a major road in New York City, with easy access from adjacent neighbourhoods including Midtown Manhattan and Central Park.

Cost:

• The procession is free for observers. There is no fee to participate in the fun unless you wish to make or purchase a bonnet, which may range in price from $10 to $200 depending on the design.

Nightlife & Entertainment

Nightlife & Entertainment in NYC

New York City is commonly referred to as "the city that never sleeps," and with cause. NYC's nightlife culture is lively, eclectic, and ever-changing, with something for everyone, whether you want world-class pubs, live music, fashionable nightclubs, or engaging shows. This is a thorough reference to New York City's nightlife and entertainment.

Bars & Pubs

What To Expect:

New York has an astounding range of bars and pubs, ranging from cosy speakeasies and rooftop lounges to vibrant sports bars and elegant cocktail lounges. Whether you want a traditional martini, artisan beer or a one-of-a-kind creation, there's a bar for you.

• Visit classic cocktail bars like The Dead Rabbit in the Financial District or Employees Only in the West Village for a fashionable atmosphere and skilfully made drinks.

• Rooftop bars in NYC are a must-see due to the city's breathtaking skyline. The Press Lounge offers amazing views of the Hudson River and Manhattan cityscape, while 230 Fifth affords outstanding views of the Empire State Building.

• Speakeasies, such as Please Don't Tell in the East Village and Apothéke in Chinatown, provide an intimate experience with speciality drinks and retro décor.

Where and when?

Bars are found across the five boroughs, with concentrations in Manhattan's Lower East Side, SoHo, Brooklyn's Williamsburg, and Queens' Astoria. Most bars open at 5:00 p.m. and remain open until 1:00 a.m. or later.

How to get there:

The underground system is the most convenient method to go about. Many bars are accessible via stations in Union Square, SoHo, Brooklyn's Williamsburg, and Lower Manhattan.

• Walking: Local neighbourhoods, such as Greenwich Village and East Village, provide easy access to nearby pubs.

Cost:

• Drink pricing might vary greatly. A beer or wine at a casual pub may cost anywhere from $5 to $10, but cocktails at more premium establishments might cost between $12 and $20. Prices for speakeasies and rooftop bars often start at about $15 per beverage.

Nightclubs and Dance Venues

What To Expect:

NYC's nightclub culture is famous, with high-energy venues offering the best DJs, themed events, and state-of-the-art sound and lighting systems. Whether you like electronic dance music (EDM), hip-hop, or indie rock, you'll find a club to suit your tastes.

• High-Energy Clubs: Marquee in Chelsea, 1 OAK in the Meatpacking District, and Lavo on the Upper East Side provide a vibrant environment with top DJs and live acts.

For a more intimate and energetic nightlife experience, check out The Apollo Theatre in Harlem for jazz and soul music or Brooklyn Steel for indie rock.

Where and when?

• Clubs and dance venues are situated in Manhattan and Brooklyn. Popular neighbourhoods include Chelsea, SoHo, East Village, and Williamsburg.

• Nightclubs normally open about 10:00 PM and host events until 4:00 AM or later, depending on the venue.

How to get there:

Underground: A convenient method to reach nightclubs and dancing venues. To get to Williamsburg, use the L train; for Chelsea and SoHo, take the A, C, or E lines.

Uber and Lyft may provide a safe and convenient choice for late-night transportation.

Cost:

• Entry prices might range from $20 to $50, depending on the location and event.

• Drink prices range from $10 to $18, with luxury bottles beginning at $300 or more.

Broadway and Off-Broadway Shows

What To Expect:

New York's theatre area is well-known for its Broadway and Off-Broadway performances. Broadway is home to some of the most renowned musicals and plays, whilst Off-Broadway features smaller, experimental, or more economical shows.

Broadway musicals such as The Lion King, Wicked, and Hamilton have high production value and engaging performances.

• For a more economical choice, Off-Broadway theatres such as The Public Theatre or The New York Theatre Workshop provide new and experimental plays and performances.

Where and when?

• Broadway theatres are mostly situated in Times Square, between 41st and 53rd Streets.

• Shows are scheduled from Tuesday to Sunday, with evening performances at 7:00 or 8:00 PM and matinees on Wednesdays, Saturdays, and Sundays at 2:00 PM.

How to get there:

Subway: Take the 1, 2, 3, N, Q, R or W line to Times Square-42nd Street. The A, C, and E trains all provide convenient access to the neighbourhood.

• Walking: Popular places like Midtown Manhattan provide easy access to the theatre sector for those staying nearby.

Cost:

- Broadway tickets normally cost $50 to $250, depending on the performance and seating area. Discounted tickets are available at TKTS booths in Times Square.

- Off-Broadway tickets often cost between $20 to $75.

Comedy Clubs

What To Expect:

New York City is a comedy hotspot, with several iconic clubs where aspiring comedians and seasoned pros perform stand-up. Expect plenty of chuckles, with presentations ranging from observational humour to political satire.

- Visit famous comedy clubs such as Comedy Cellar in Greenwich Village, Carolines on Broadway, or Stand Up NY for an amazing night of humour.

Where and when?

- Comedy clubs may be found around Manhattan, particularly in Greenwich Village, East Village, and Times Square.

- When: Shows typically begin at 8:00 PM, with late-night options at 10:30 PM or later on weekends.

How to get there:

Underground: Greenwich Village is accessible by the F, A, C or E trains, while Times Square is served by the N, Q, R or W lines.

- Walking: Clubs in Greenwich Village and East Village are conveniently located nearby.

Cost:

- Cover rates vary from $10 and $25, with drink minimums of $10 to $20 per person.

Late Night Dining and Food Trucks

What To Expect:

The party does not stop when the pubs and clubs shut. New York is well-known for its late-night food culture, with food trucks and restaurants providing anything from pizza slices to dim sum at all hours.

- Late-Night Eateries: Try Joe's Pizza or Halal Guys' street cuisine around midnight. For a more substantial meal, visit Katz's Delicatessen (open 24 hours a day, seven days a week) for their famed pastrami sandwich.

Where and when?

- Hotspots for late-night dining in NYC include the Lower East Side, Midtown, and Greenwich Village.

Food trucks often operate from late evening until early morning, particularly on weekends.

How to get there:

• Walking: Food trucks and cafes are conveniently accessible near nightclubs and bars.

Subway stations, like 14th Street-Union Square and Times Square, are near food truck centres.

Cost:

Food truck meals, such as gyros or falafel, often cost between $5 and $12. A late-night restaurant dinner might cost between $10 and $20.

New York City's nightlife and entertainment alternatives are sure to delight any kind of night bird. Whether you're looking for an elegant cocktail experience, an exciting nightlife, a world-class Broadway production, or plain old-fashioned comedy, NYC has it all. With so many alternatives, each night in the city seems like a fresh new experience waiting to be discovered.

Chapter 12. Tips For A Memorable Trip

Safety and Etiquette

Safety and Etiquette in New York City.

New York City is renowned for its colourful environment, fast-paced lifestyle, and diversified population. While it is typically a safe and inviting environment for guests, being aware of safety considerations and adhering to local etiquette can assist in guaranteeing a pleasant and pleasurable time.

Safety Tips

Stay aware of your surroundings.

NYC is brimming with vitality, and it's easy to get caught in the sights and noises. However, it is critical to be aware, particularly in busy areas. Keep an eye on your stuff and use caution while using your phone or other technological devices in public. Avoid flaunting pricey jewellery or cameras in less populated locations.

Use public transport wisely.

New York's public transit system is secure, but it might be scary if you're not acquainted with it.

Underground: Use well-lit locations, particularly at night, and avoid empty vehicles. If possible, wait for a train in a more crowded car.

• Buses are normally safe but be aware of pickpockets while getting on and off.

• Always use a licensed taxi or ridesharing vehicle. Before entering a rideshare car, make sure the license plate and driver's name match those on the app.

Avoid sketchy areas late at night.

New York, like any other big metropolis, has neighbourhoods that may be less secure after dark. While most regions of Manhattan are well-patrolled, it's best to avoid less populous places, particularly in the outlying boroughs such as the Bronx and some portions of Brooklyn and Queens. Always use care while travelling alone at night.

Know emergency numbers.

In the event of an emergency, call 911 for police, fire, or medical help. Many streets and subways include emergency call boxes. Most tube stations also have personnel ready to help.

Keep an eye out for traffic.

While New York is a pedestrian-friendly city, it still has a lot of fast-moving traffic. Always utilise crosswalks and wait for the green light before crossing the street, even if traffic seems to be stopped. Be extra careful while going through congested areas like Times Square or Fifth Avenue, where traffic may be unexpected.

Avoid street scams.

Be aware of street entertainers, sellers, or those who seek money or initiate uninvited talks. Common scams include "blessing" someone with a "good luck charm" and then requesting money in exchange. If you feel uncomfortable, politely refuse and move away.

Know Where the Nearest Police Station is.

Learn the locations of surrounding police stations. They may be found on most maps and applications. If you lose anything or feel frightened, knowing where the closest station is might be useful.

Etiquette in New York City.

Maintain Your Personal Space.

New Yorkers are accustomed to crowds and cramped areas, but it's still crucial to respect personal space. Avoid going too near to people on the metro, buses, or in lines, particularly if it is packed. A little patience and respect for personal space will go a long way.

Walk with purpose.

In New York, people walk quickly. When going along the street, keep up with the flow and attempt to remain to the right on pavements, particularly when entering doors or crossing streets. If you need to glance at your map or snap a picture, move aside to avoid impeding pedestrian traffic.

Queue Up Politely.

New Yorkers anticipate orderly lineups, particularly on the tube, in ticket queues and at shops. Always wait your turn and avoid cutting in line. Even at Shake Shack and Eataly, skipping the wait is considered impolite.

Use headphones in public places.

While you may want to listen to music or a podcast on the road, remember to wear headphones in public places. It is basic decency not to bother individuals around you with music or personal calls.

Respect the "No Talking" Rule in Some Places.

Some New Yorkers like quiet time, particularly in public places such as libraries, museums, and cafés. Avoid speaking loudly on your phone or in gatherings where others expect to be quiet.

Tipping

Tipping is usual in New York City and is anticipated in a variety of service settings.

• Restaurants often charge 15-20% of the bill.

- Taxis/rideshares charge 10-15% of the fare.

- Hotel staff: Tip $1-$2 per bag for bellhops and $1-$2 per night for cleaning.

Be polite in crowded areas.

New Yorkers are renowned for being straightforward and speedy, but they also value civility. If you need to ask someone for directions or help, approach them gently and briefly. Most New Yorkers will be courteous provided you respect their time.

Do not stand in the middle of the sidewalk.

When going throughout the city, particularly in congested places, avoid blocking the flow of foot traffic. If you need to halt, go to the side of the sidewalk to prevent blocking other people's path.

Do not take pictures without permission.

While shooting the skyline or landmarks is usual, please respect people's privacy. Avoid taking photos of individuals without their consent, particularly in more intimate situations such as restaurants, cafés, and concerts.

Public Behaviour

Public shows of love are typically acceptable in New York City, but it is vital to consider the context and environment. Loud disagreements or too enthusiastic behaviour in public places might draw unwelcome attention, so always use caution.

New York City is an exciting location to visit, but like every large city, it has its own set of safety precautions and etiquette to guarantee that inhabitants and visitors can live peacefully. Staying aware of your surroundings, respecting others' space, and following local traditions can allow you to make the most of your NYC journey while also adding to the city's distinct energy and charm.

Budget-Friendly Travel Tips:

Budget-Friendly Travel Tips for NYC

New York City may be a costly visit, but there are several ways to enjoy all of the sights, restaurants, and activities without breaking the bank. Whether you're a first-time visitor or a seasoned traveller, here are some budget-friendly travel tips:

Use public transportation.

The underground and buses are the most cost-effective transportation options in New York. A MetroCard provides unlimited access to the underground and buses, saving you money over individual tickets. A 7-day unlimited ticket costs roughly $33, providing you with a week's worth of travel at a fraction of the cost of taxis or rideshares.

• Many prominent sights in NYC are easily accessible by foot. This is an excellent method to tour neighbourhoods and see the city without spending money on transportation.

Take advantage of free attractions.

• Central Park provides many activities like strolling, picnics, bird-watching, and people-watching. There is also free entertainment, such as summer concerts and activities.

• Some New York institutions, including The Met, MoMA, and the American Museum of Natural History, have a "pay-what-you-wish" entrance policy on specific days and hours. Check for these possibilities, since you may visit these cultural sites for a fraction of the typical cost.

• Walking over the Brooklyn Bridge provides stunning vistas of Manhattan and Brooklyn and is entirely free. It's an excellent opportunity to see one of New York City's most iconic buildings while saving money.

Take advantage of discounted passes.

Purchase a New York City Pass, Explorer Pass, or Go City Card to save money on entry to popular sights such as the Empire State Building, Statue of Liberty, and Top of the Rock. These passes may help you save up to 40% off normal entrance fees.

• Discounted Broadway tickets are available at the TKTS Booth in Times Square, offering up to 50% off same-day performances. In addition, go online for special bargains or lotteries for famous performances.

Eat like a local.

• Street Food: New York's food trucks and sellers provide inexpensive, genuine meals. From hot dogs and pretzels to gyros and falafel, you can have a delicious meal for a few bucks.

• Budget-Friendly Restaurants: NYC offers several economical eating alternatives. Chinatown has some of the greatest and cheapest cuisines, with restaurants like Xi'an Famous Foods and Joe's Shanghai delivering full meals for around $10. Additionally, visit Gray's Papaya for an iconic, low-cost hot dog experience.

• Bars and restaurants often offer happy hour deals, including cheap beverages and appetisers. Taking advantage of these bargains allows you to taste some of the city's best drinks or beers without going over budget.

Stay at budget-friendly accommodations.

• Affordable hostels in New York, such as HI NYC Hostel and The Local NYC in Long Island City, provide shared dormitories or individual rooms at a lower rate than hotels. Furthermore, inexpensive hotel businesses such as Pod Hotels and The Jane Hotel provide trendy but economical accommodations.

• Use Airbnb or similar services to rent homes or rooms in less touristic regions, saving money on housing and exploring local neighbourhoods. Booking in advance might help you get the greatest discounts.

Plan your trip at off-peak times.

• Travel during the off-season to avoid expensive rates for flights, accommodation, and attractions. Visiting throughout the winter (excluding holidays), early spring, and autumn will allow you to avoid crowds and get cheaper discounts.

• To ensure the best rates, book your journey in advance since airfare prices frequently vary. Using airline comparison services such as Google Flights or Skyscanner might help you identify low-cost choices.

Free or Discounted Events

• Free Outdoor Events: NYC hosts several free outdoor concerts, festivals, and events. For example, Shakespeare in the Park in Central Park and free summer concerts in Brooklyn Bridge Park are excellent opportunities to enjoy the arts without paying a fee.

• Check local event lists, such as Time Out New York or NYCgo, for free or low-cost events in the city.

Shop Smart.

• Discount retailers in New York, such as Century 21 and TJ Maxx, offer reduced pricing on designer names. For unique and inexpensive souvenirs, visit Canal Street for deals on jewellery, clothing, and electronics.

• Thrift shops and flea markets in NYC, such as Beacon's Closet and Buffalo Exchange, offer high-quality clothing and accessories at a lower cost than new. Flea markets, like Brooklyn Flea and Artists & Fleas, provide unique finds at reasonable prices.

Take advantage of free walking tours.

• Several companies provide free walking tours of NYC neighbourhoods. While these tours are free to attend, it is customary to tip the guide based on your experiences. These tours are an excellent way to learn about the city's history and culture without having to pay for a costly guided tour.

Be Strategic With Your Sightseeing

• Research: Popular NYC attractions may be pricey. However, by doing preliminary study, you may prioritise the activities that are most important to you while avoiding those that may not be as vital. If you want to visit everything, consider grouping attractions with discounted passes.

Group neighbouring attractions together to save money on transit and make the most of your time. For example, you might go to Central Park in the morning, wander around Fifth Avenue, and then tour adjacent museums like the Empire State Building in the afternoon.

Travelling to New York City on a budget is quite achievable with some preparation and imagination. By using public transit, visiting free sights, taking advantage of discounts, and being wise about where you stay and eat, you can enjoy the best of the Big Apple without overpaying.

Chapter 13. Frequently Asked Questions

Common Queries About NYC Travel

Common Queries About NYC Travel

New York City may be intimidating for first-time visitors owing to its vast size, numerous attractions, and distinct culture. Here are some commonly asked questions (FAQs) to assist you explore the city and make your vacation more enjoyable:

Is New York City Safe for Tourists?

New York City is typically secure for visitors, but like any large city, it's crucial to keep vigilant of your surroundings, particularly in busy places or new districts. Stay in well-lit places at night, avoid secluded streets, and be wary of pickpockets. Popular tourist destinations like Times Square and Central Park are typically secure during the day, although certain districts in Brooklyn and The Bronx may be less appealing to visitors after dark.

How can I get about New York City?

The easiest method to travel to NYC is to use public transit, notably the underground and buses, which are both inexpensive and widespread. Taxis and ridesharing services such as Uber and Lyft are also commonly accessible, albeit they may be more costly, particularly during peak hours. Walking is another excellent option to see the city since most sights are within walking distance of one another.

What is the best time of year to visit New York City?

The ideal time to visit New York City depends on your choices.

Spring (April-June) and Fall (September-November) provide milder weather, fewer visitors, and beautiful colours in parks.

Summer (July and August) is a popular time for outdoor activities, but it may be congested and costly.

• The winter season (December-February) is chilly yet wonderful, particularly around the holidays with decorations, ice skating, and fewer visitors.

Should I tip in New York City?

Tipping is customary in NYC and is expected in many situations.

• At restaurants, tip between 15% and 20% of the total bill (before taxes).

• For taxis and rideshares, tip between 10% and 20% of the fare.

• For hotel staff, tip $1 to $2 per bag for bellhops and $1 to $5 per night for housekeepers.

• For guided tours, a tip of $5-10 per person is appreciated.

How Can I Save Money in NYC?

There are several ways to save money in NYC.

• Use public transportation: The subway and buses are affordable and can connect you to most major attractions.

• Look for discounts, such as free museum admission, happy hour specials, and free outdoor concerts and festivals.

• Save money by staying in budget accommodations such as hostels, Airbnb rentals, or hotels.

• Consider eating at food trucks or local eateries for more affordable meals.

What Are the Must-See NYC Attractions?

Some of the top attractions in New York City are:

• The Statue of Liberty and Ellis Island.

Locations include the Empire State Building, Central Park, and Times Square.

• Broadway Shows

• The Metropolitan Museum of Art • 9/11 Memorial and Museum

• Brooklyn Bridge.

There's so much more to discover, but here are a few attractions that should be on your schedule.

Can I walk anywhere in New York City?

New York is one of the world's most walkable cities, with numerous important attractions within walking distance of one another. Walking is an excellent method to explore neighbourhoods such as Greenwich Village, SoHo, and Chinatown. However, New York City is incredibly huge, and the underground provides a speedy and inexpensive means to go great distances.

Is There Anything Free to Do in NYC?

Yes, there are many free activities to do in New York City:

• Central Park offers summer activities such as picnics and free concerts.

• Free Staten Island Ferry rides provide breathtaking views of the Statue of Liberty and the Manhattan skyline.

• Walking over the Brooklyn Bridge is free and offers stunning views of the city.

• Museums: Some museums, like The Museum at the Fashion Institute of Technology (FIT) and The National Museum of the American Indian, provide free entrance with recommended contributions.

How Do I Get Broadway Show Tickets?

There are various methods to get tickets for Broadway shows:

• TKTS Booths, located in Times Square, provide cheap tickets for same-day shows (up to 50% off).

• Online: TodayTix, Broadway.com, and Ticketmaster have advance ticketing options, however savings may be limited.

• Lottery Tickets: Some Broadway plays offer cheap tickets via lotteries that may be entered in person or online.

How Can I Stay Connected in New York City?

To remain connected in NYC, many public venues, cafés, and restaurants have free Wi-Fi. Many parks and tube stations also provide free Wi-Fi.

To remain connected when travelling from overseas, try purchasing a local SIM card or renting a portable Wi-Fi hotspot.

Is NYC Expensive?

Yes, New York City can be pricey, particularly when it comes to lodging and eating. However, with proper planning, you may visit the city on a budget. To save money, utilise public transportation, stay at low-cost hotels or hostels, visit free attractions, and eat at local restaurants and food trucks.

Can I visit New York City in one day?

While one day is not enough to see all New York City has to offer, you can still visit the highlights. A typical one-day schedule would include a stop at the Statue of Liberty, a stroll around Central Park, a tour of Times Square, and an evening Broadway musical. Make the most of your time by planning and prioritising your must-see destinations.

Which Neighbourhoods Should I Visit?

NYC is divided into five boroughs: Manhattan, Brooklyn, Queens, The Bronx, and Staten Island. Each has its particular atmosphere and attractions:

Manhattan is the city's core, with renowned monuments such as Times Square, Central Park, and Broadway. Brooklyn is known for its artsy ambience, historic neighbourhoods like DUMBO, and the gorgeous Brooklyn Bridge.

• Queens: Enjoy ethnic variety, international food, and attractions like Flushing Meadows-Corona Park. • The Bronx: Explore the Bronx Zoo, Yankee Stadium, and the New York Botanical Garden. • Staten Island: Famous for the Staten Island Ferry and peaceful residential neighbourhoods.

What are the best souvenirs to buy in New York City?

Popular souvenirs from New York City include I Love NY T-shirts, replicas of the Statue of Liberty, street art from local galleries or markets, unique jewellery from thrift stores and boutiques, and NYC-themed cuisine such as bagels, pretzels, or chocolate.

Can I drink NYC tap water?

Yes, New York City's tap water is regarded as one of the finest in the nation and is completely safe to drink. Many residents carry reusable water bottles that they may refill for free at water fountains or eateries.

Whether you're visiting New York City for the first time or returning for another adventure, these frequently asked questions can help you plan a seamless, pleasurable trip. With a little preparation, you'll be able to traverse the city like an expert and enjoy all the Big Apple has to offer!

Chapter 14. Conclusion

Final Tips for Exploring the City

New York City might be intimidating, but with a little planning, you can make the most of your stay in a city that never sleeps. Here are some last recommendations to help you have a great experience:

Plan, but leave room for spontaneity.

While an itinerary is useful, avoid overscheduling oneself. New York is a vibrant city, and part of its allure is uncovering hidden treasures as you go. Whether it's stumbling into a street artist in SoHo, discovering a terrific restaurant in Chinatown, or visiting a quiet part of Central Park, allowing some free time in your day allows for unexpected excursions.

Dress Comfortably.

You will be walking a lot, so wear comfortable shoes. Sneakers are an excellent choice, and consider bringing a small backpack with basics such as drinks, sunscreen and your phone. Be cautious of the weather—bring layers in the winter, a decent umbrella in the spring and autumn, and light clothes with sunscreen in the summer.

Use the Subway app.

The New York Subway might seem daunting, but it's the most efficient way to travel about the city. Download a metro map app, such as Citymapper or Google Maps, to help you navigate the subway system effectively. The app will also notify you of delays or service changes.

Stay hydrated, and take breaks.

New York is crowded and fast-paced, so it's important to remain hydrated and take pauses as required. There are several water fountains around the city, and many cafés and restaurants provide complimentary water with each meal. Take a break at one of the city's parks, such as Bryant Park or Washington Square Park, to recharge your batteries.

Be aware of your surroundings.

Though New York place is a generally secure place, you should constantly be vigilant of your surroundings. Keep your possessions safe in busy locations such as Times Square or subways, since pickpockets may be a problem. Avoid appearing lost on your map; if you need directions, ask a local.

Do not be afraid to ask for help.

New Yorkers are often busy, but they are also kind and eager to assist if asked. If you need directions, restaurant suggestions or tube guidance, don't be afraid to start up a conversation. Most locals are ready to offer their thoughts and insights.

Take advantage of the city passes and discounts.

If you want to visit numerous sites, consider getting a New York City Pass or a New York Pass, which provides savings and skip-the-line admission to popular sights such as the Empire State Building, Top of the Rock, and the Metropolitan Museum of Art. Furthermore, many museums provide free admission on certain days or periods, so check their websites in advance.

Be prepared for crowds.

New York is often congested, particularly in prominent places such as Times Square or during major events. Be prepared to face crowds, particularly around rush hour. To avoid crowds, visit popular attractions early in the morning or late in the evening.

Explore Beyond Manhattan

Manhattan is the centre of New York City, but do not neglect the other boroughs. Brooklyn has stunning vistas and trendy neighbourhoods such as DUMBO and Williamsburg. Queens has amazing culinary and cultural variety, while The Bronx has green places such as The New York Botanical Garden and The Bronx Zoo. Each borough has its distinct character and is worth investigating.

Embrace Public Transportation

The underground, buses, and ferries provide very efficient modes of transportation across the city. Taxis and ridesharing services are handy, but they may be expensive, particularly during peak hours. Get a MetroCard for convenient access to the tube and buses, and use a navigation app to keep track of your itinerary and prevent getting lost.

Expect the unexpected.

New York place is a place of surprises, and things seldom go as expected. Whether it's attending a pop-up event or seeing a street performer on Broadway, accept the unexpected. Some of the finest experiences in NYC result from being open to new chances that emerge during the day.

Enjoy the food, but watch your budget.

New York is a foodie's paradise, yet it's easy to splurge, particularly when eating at fancy restaurants. To stay within your budget, consider local street cuisine from food trucks, casual restaurants, or one of Brooklyn's numerous inexpensive markets, such as Chelsea Market or Smorgasburg. The city offers possibilities at all price levels.

Get the whole New York City experience, not just the tourist experience.

While seeing the great sites is vital, don't overlook the local experiences that contribute to New York's appeal. Explore neighbourhoods including Greenwich Village, East Village, and Chinatown. Try an underground speakeasy or see an off-Broadway performance. It is the little details that will make your vacation memorable.

Keep some flexibility in your schedule.

New York City has a lot to offer, but you may not be able to accomplish everything you desire. Keep your schedule flexible so that you may take advantage of opportunities as they arise. The city is continually changing, so there's always something new to explore.

Take time to just watch and listen.

Finally, take a few seconds to relax and enjoy the view of the city. Whether it's people-watching in Union Square, enjoying a rooftop bar view, or seeing the skyline from the Staten Island Ferry, New York's liveliness is one of its most recognisable characteristics. Relax, take in the rush and bustle, and enjoy being a part of the city's distinct pulse.

Bonus

Bonus: Expert Photography Tips

Capturing delightful moments in New York City is essential for remembering your visit. This extra area provides expert photography methods to assist readers and visitors capture stunning photographs of famous landmarks, bustling neighbourhoods, and one-of-a-kind experiences. Whether you're shooting with a professional camera or a smartphone, these guidelines will help you make the most of natural light, composition, and timing, ensuring that your images capture the genuine spirit of the city. From composing the ideal image of the Empire State Building at sunset to catching the busy streets of Times Square, these professional tips will help you wonderfully capture your NYC memories.

Expert Photography Tips to Capture Beautiful Moments in New York City

New York City is full of breathtaking views, and as a visitor, you will want to capture every moment. Whether you're using a high-end camera or a smartphone, here are some expert photography tips to help you create stunning, memorable images.

Golden Hour Magic

The "golden hour" is the time shortly after dawn and before sunset when the light is soft and warm, offering great circumstances for outdoor photography. This is the best moment to snap monuments like the Statue of Liberty or the skyline from Brooklyn Bridge Park. The warm warmth of the sunshine makes the city's structures and streets appear even more lovely.

Use the Rule of Thirds

To generate more dynamic and visually attractive images, employ the rule of thirds. Imagine splitting your frame into a 3x3 grid. Place the primary subject—whether it's a landmark, person, or street scene—along these lines or at the intersections. This generates equilibrium and attracts the viewer's attention naturally through the picture.

Focus on Composition

Look for unique perspectives, patterns, and lines to make your photograph stand out. The Brooklyn Bridge is a perfect example, where you can play with perspectives—shooting through the bridge's complex cables or catching it from below. The geometric features of New York City architecture, such as the sharp angles of The Vessel in Hudson Yards, may also create appealing compositions.

Capture the Energy of the Streets

New York is recognised for its fast-paced and lively vitality. To capture the spirit of this, try motion blur. A long exposure photo of a busy street, for example, may capture the movement of yellow taxis, walkers, and bicycles while keeping the city skyline in focus. A tripod is necessary for this procedure.

Get close to your subject.

Don't be scared to approach your subject, particularly while capturing street art, marketplaces, or food. Close-up images show delicate details, such as the feel of a food truck bagel or graffiti art in Bushwick, Brooklyn. Zooming in on details will allow your images to convey a unique tale.

Use Reflections to Your Advantage

New York has abundant shiny surfaces, ranging from puddles after rainfall to glass towers. Use these reflections to enhance the depth and originality of your images. The reflections of skyscrapers on Central Park's glass windows, or the shimmering lights of Times Square on a damp roadway, may create an eye-catching sight.

Incorporate People and Local Culture.

To fully portray the essence of New York, incorporate both natives and visitors in your photographs. Street performers in Washington Square Park, a food seller in Chinatown, and motorcyclists on the Brooklyn Bridge all offer character and perspective to your photographs. To capture real moments, take candid photographs rather than staged ones.

Play with light and shadows.

New York's high-rise skyscrapers cast spectacular shadows, particularly at dawn and twilight. Use shadows to frame your subjects, or play with light contrast to emphasise certain portions of your photograph. For example, photographing the One World Trade Centre against a deep blue sky at twilight might result in spectacular silhouettes.

Try night photography.

New York City never sleeps, and its lights come on at night. A tripod may help keep your camera stable at night, particularly in low-light circumstances. To highlight the city's energy, focus on renowned places at night, such as Times Square, the Empire State Building, or the Brooklyn Bridge. To avoid picture noise, ensure that your camera's ISO is properly adjusted.

Do Not Forget About Smartphone Photography.

Modern smartphones have powerful cameras, so don't underestimate their capabilities. Use your phone's portrait mode to get excellent focus on subjects and gorgeous background blur, particularly when capturing food or street photos. Also, explore with panoramic images to capture expansive vistas such as those from the Top of the Rock or Central Park.

Use leading lines.

Leading lines guide the viewer's eye throughout the shot. Look for lines that direct the viewer's attention, such as subway platforms, trails through Central Park, or the streets of Manhattan. These lines give your images a feeling of depth and perspective, making them more intriguing.

Capture New York's unique weather conditions.

Every season and weather condition in NYC provides a unique picture opportunity. Rain may add atmosphere to your photos by casting reflections and catching the shine on the pavement. Snow, albeit uncommon, may convert the city into a winter paradise. Sunny days provide a vibrant environment, ideal for capturing the city's liveliness. Keep an eye on the forecast so you can take advantage of changing weather.

Useful website.

Official New York City Tourism Website.

• Website address: www.nycgo.com.

• The official tourist site for NYC provides thorough information on sights, events, itineraries, and more.

The NYC Department of Transportation (MTA)

• Website address: www.mta.info.

• Contact:

• Call 511 (inside New York).

• Outside NYC: +1 (718) 330-1234.

• Information about subway, bus, and rail services, including timetables and updates.

New York City Police Department (NYPD) Non-emergency

• Website address: www.nyc.gov/html/nypd.

• Contact:

• Non-emergency number: +1 (212) 694-9794.

• For general enquiries, email info@nypd.org.

Description: Non-emergency assistance and crime prevention resources.

New York City 311

• Website: www.nyc.gov/311.

• Call 311 (in NYC) or +1 (212) 639-9675 (outside NYC).

• Description: City services and information, including sanitation and public aid.

The Statue of Liberty and Ellis Island

• Website: www.statueoflibertytickets.com.

• Phone: +1 (877) 523-9849.

• Purchase ferry tickets to the Statue of Liberty and Ellis Island. Find more about visiting hours and guided tours.

New York City Airport Information

• JFK Airport (John F. Kennedy)

• Website address: www.jfkairport.com.

• Phone: +1 (718) 244-4444.

• LaGuardia Airport (LGA)

• Website address: www.laguardiaairport.com.

• Phone: +1 (718) 533-3988.

• Newark Liberty International Airport (EWR)

• Website address: www.newarkairport.com.

• Phone: +1 (973) 961-6000.

Airport information includes terminals, transit choices, and flight status.

NYC Ferry

• Website address: www.ferry.nyc.

• Phone: +1 (718) 390-2345.

• Information about NYC's ferry service, linking Manhattan, Brooklyn, Queens, and Staten Island.

The Metropolitan Museum of Art (the Met)

• Website: www.metmuseum.org.

• Phone number: +1 (212) 535-7710.

• Provides information about exhibitions, opening hours, and tickets for The Met's many sites.

The Museum of Modern Art (MoMA)

• Website address: www.moma.org.

• Phone: +1 (212) 708-9400.

• Detailed information on the museum, including hours of operation and ticket sales.

New York City Pass

• Website: www.citypass.com/New-York.

• Phone number: +1 (888) 330-5008.

Description: Provides reduced tickets to popular sights such as the Empire State Building, The Met, and Top of the Rock.

New York City Public Library

• Website address: www.nypl.org.

• Phone: +1 (212) 340-0849.

• Description: Library locations, hours, and programming. A fantastic location for peaceful time and study.

NYC Transit Authority Lost and Found

• Website address: www.mta.info/lostandfound

• Call +1 (877) 699-4277.

• Report and enquire about missing things on subways, buses, and commuter trains.

Times Square Information Centre

• Website address: www.timessquarenyc.org.

• Phone: +1 (212) 768-1560.

• The official website for visiting Times Square provides tourist information, events, and suggestions.

New York Public Library's Information Desk

• Website address: www.nypl.org.

• Phone: +1 (917) 275-6975.

• Description: Offers resources for events, exhibits, books, and digital content.

New York City's Department of Health

• Website address: www.nyc.gov/health.

• Phone: +1 (212) 639-9675.

• Health and safety guidelines for travellers, addressing current health issues (e.g. COVID-19 protocols).

Dear Readers,

First and foremost, I'd like to express my heartfelt gratitude to you for choosing to embark on this journey through the pages of New York City Travel Guide: Experience the Best of NYC Adventures. It has been a labour of love, and I hope that the information, tips, and insights contained within these pages will allow you to experience the magic of New York City in ways you never imagined.

Writing this guide took more than just research; it required dedication, countless hours, and significant personal resources to ensure that every detail was correct and every recommendation was genuine. I travelled throughout the city, visited landmarks, discovered hidden gems, and interviewed locals and experts to create the most comprehensive guide possible. This investment of time, energy, and money was made with one goal in mind: to provide you with the best possible experience while exploring the Big Apple.

Your feedback is invaluable. As a travel guide writer, each review and comment you leave has a direct impact on my development and helps me improve my work. Your positive review may direct others to this book, while your constructive criticism may influence future editions to better serve travellers like you. Your thoughts reflect the effort I put into this book, and knowing that it helped you enjoy your time in New York City brings me great joy.

I firmly think that the experience does not stop when you shut the book; rather, it continues as you explore, learn, and create memories in one of the world's most exciting cities. If this guide made your stay more pleasurable, efficient, or enlightening, I would be glad if you could take the time to provide feedback. Your remarks are the gasoline that propels me ahead, always seeking to make each subsequent effort better and more useful.

Thank you for believing in this guide and supporting my job as a writer. It means more to me than words can explain.

I wish you all the best in your New York City experience!

Warm regards.

Carole J. Harvey

Printed in Great Britain
by Amazon